Florida A&M University, Tallahassee
Florida Atlantic University, Boca Raton
Florida Gulf Coast University, Ft. Myers
Florida International University, Miami
Florida State University, Tallahassee
University of Central Florida, Orlando
University of Florida, Gainesville
University of North Florida, Jacksonville
University of South Florida, Tampa
University of West Florida, Pensacola

The Evolution of *Converso* Literature

The Writings of the Converted Jews
of Medieval Spain

Gregory B. Kaplan

University Press of Florida

Gainesville · Tallahassee · Tampa · Boca Raton
Pensacola · Orlando · Miami · Jacksonville · Ft. Myers

07 06 05 04 03 02   6 5 4 3 2 1

Library of Congress Cataloging-in-Publication Data
Kaplan, Gregory B., 1966–
The evolution of converso literature: the writings of the converted Jews
of medieval Spain / Gregory B. Kaplan
p. cm.
Includes bibliographical references (p.) and index.
ISBN 0-8130-2475-7
1. Spanish literature—To 1500—History and criticism. 2. Spanish
literature—Jewish authors—History and criticism. 3. Christian converts
from Judaism—Spain—History. 4. Discrimination in literature. 5. Outsiders
in literature. 6. Politics and literature—Spain. 7. Literature and society—
Spain. 8. Spain—Intellectual life—711–1516. I. Title.
PQ6060.K36   2002
860.9'8924—dc21   2001053515

The University Press of Florida is the scholarly publishing agency
for the State University System of Florida, comprising Florida A&M
University, Florida Atlantic University, Florida Gulf Coast University,
Florida International University, Florida State University, University of
Central Florida, University of Florida, University of North Florida,
University of South Florida, and University of West Florida.

University Press of Florida
15 Northwest 15th Street
Gainesville, FL 32611–2079
http://www.upf.com

For Nuria

Contents

Preface

This book is intended to serve as a comprehensive guide to the evolution of *converso* literature from the 1460s until 1499. In it I strive to analyze that corpus of literature by considering both *converso* history and semiotic principles of literary discourse. Although this book is intended primarily for specialists in medieval Spanish literature, readers interested in Judaic studies, Hispanic poetry in general, or European social conflicts in the fifteenth and sixteenth centuries may also find it useful.

I am grateful to the individuals who have helped me complete this project. For their advice and friendship, I wish to thank Eric and Kasandra Atwood, Dr. Cynthia Duncan, Dr. Michael Handelsman, Dr. Irene Mizrahi, the staff of the John C. Hodges Library at the University of Tennessee, and my editors at the University Press of Florida, Judy Goffman and Amy Gorelick. For their numerous suggestions and careful readings of my manuscript, I owe special debts of gratitude to Dr. George Greenia and Dr. Denise DiPuccio. I could not have begun this project without the encouragement of my parents, Dr. Marvin Kaplan and Deborah Zelizer Kaplan, Esq. Words cannot express my gratitude to my wife, Dr. Nuria Cruz-Cámara, without whom I could not have completed this book.

Shorter versions of Chapters 4 ("Toward the Establishment"), 5 ("In Search of Salvation"), and 6 ("Rodrigo Cota's 'Diálogo'") have laid the groundwork for my present conclusions. I wish to thank *La corónica*, *Hispanic Review*, and *Indiana Journal of Hispanic Literatures*, respectively, for allowing me to incorporate this material into the present study. Sections of Chapters 1 and 3 are included in an article published in *Quaderni ibero-americani* ("'Como non deben seer apremiados los judíos'"), which focuses on a theme (the legal precedent for the Sentencia-Estatuto of 1449) that is related to (but beyond the scope of) this book. I would also like to express my appreciation to *Quaderni ibero-americani* for granting me permission to incorporate these sections. Funding for the preparation of the index was provided by the University of Tennessee Exhibit, Performance, and Publication Expense Fund.

Abbreviations

B.C.E.	Before the Common Era
c.	circa
Exod.	Exodus
Gal.	Galatians
Gen.	Genesis
r.	reigned
st.	stanza(s)
v.	verse(s)

Introduction

In some respects the topics studied here spring from the lively debate produced by the publication in *La corónica* (fall 1996) of a critical cluster that focused on the textual nature of the *"converso* voice" (Hutcheson 3). The essays in that cluster, including my own ("Toward the Establishment of a Christian Identity"), demonstrate the heterogeneity of this voice. The concept of a *converso* literature can no longer be explained in essentialist terms that insinuate a uniform expression of despair or protest. The diversity of the *conversos* themselves, and in particular those of Castile, the region with the largest *converso* community (upon whose literature this book focuses), prevents such a strict definition. At the same time, certain events clearly mark the trajectory by which these New Christians came to be alienated from Old Christian Spanish society. Although individual *conversos* were alienated in varying degrees, it is the premise of this book that conclusions may be reached regarding the nature of this two-tiered Christianity by thoroughly examining the influence of these events on literary texts.

As Dayle Seidenspinner-Núñez observes in her contribution to the critical cluster, "The real challenge for *converso* studies is to explore the full complexity and range of the *converso* presence in late medieval and early modern Spain" (7). Early efforts at approaching the topic, whether favorable or unfavorable toward the idea that literature reflects the contemporary social dichotomy between Old and New Christians, did not touch upon the nature of this complexity. Américo Castro, in his conception of a "tradición sombría" (somber tradition) in *converso* letters (*La realidad* 534), an idea elaborated and amplified in several of his books, implicitly advocated the existence of a *converso* literature without identifying its distinguishing features. Although Castro's theories laid the foundation for future studies of the *converso* presence in literature, his tendency to essentialize the historical trajectory of the *converso* plight inspired acerbic responses by his detractors, namely Claudio Sánchez-Albornoz and Eugenio Asensio. But in refuting Castro's "tradición sombría" these detractors also failed to consider the works in question within their particular historical contexts. While scholars such as Stephen Gilman, Francisco Márquez Villanueva, Julio Rodríguez Puértolas, and Kenneth Scholberg have provided much support for Castro by analyzing many facets of the depiction of the marginalized *converso,* a comprehensive study of the evolution of their literary voices has yet to be produced.

A number of past studies of literary representations of *conversos* (including my own) have not thoroughly addressed two issues that must be discussed in light of their complex history, namely, the conception of a *converso* and the notion of a *converso* text. With regard to the former, socioeconomic and religious differences among individuals demand a broad vision. Recent studies by David Gitlitz and José Faur strive to clarify the issue by providing *converso* typologies. According to Gitlitz, "While there is a good deal of variance according to time and place, *conversos* can generally be thought of in four broad groups according to their self-concept. Some thought of themselves as (1) Christians; some as (2) Jews; some as (3) seekers of truth caught between two religions; and some as (4) skeptical dropouts, for whom religion was as unimportant as the times allowed it to be" (84). Faur also finds four types of *conversos*: "Ideologically, the *converso* population may be divided into four classes: those who wanted to be Christians and have nothing to do with Judaism, those who wanted to be Jewish and have nothing to do with Christianity, those who wanted to be both, and those who wanted to be neither" (41).

Ideologically, many of the *conversos* I consider appear to fit into the first category defined by Gitlitz (*conversos* who thought of themselves as Christians), and in particular into one of four subgroups within this category, which Gitlitz labels "Christian reformers" (85):

> Some new-Christians, persuaded to convert by an idealized vision of Catholicism, were acutely disappointed by what they found to be discriminatory practices of the Church, particularly the Inquisition and the purity-of-blood laws. . . . The distinguishing characteristic of this group of *conversos* is their compulsion to express their dissatisfaction with the status quo. . . . [Included] are many of the Spanish late-medieval and Golden Age writers in whose works run strong thematic currents of tolerance, equity, and profound unease with current governmental, religious and societal practices. In this group one might consider . . . Antón Montoro, Juan de Valladolid, Rodrigo de

Cota, Juan Álvarez Gato, and many other late fifteenth-century "songbook" (*cancionero*) poets. . . . [in addition to] Diego de San Pedro, [and] Fernando de Rojas." (85–86)

Although Faur does not specifically mention many of the *converso* writers whom I consider, as Gitlitz does in this passage, in assessing the ideologies of "some of the most distinguished thinkers of the time" (45) he identifies the "faithful Christian *converso*," who "wanted to assimilate into the Christian body and lose all contacts with Judaism. . . . [in order] to avoid the massacres and persecutions of Christianity" (43). Like the "Christian reformers" described by Gitlitz, these "faithful Christian *conversos*" were disillusioned that Christian society was unwilling to accept them, in spite of the fact that they were Christians.

The typologies offered by Faur and Gitlitz are useful tools for understanding the diversity of the *converso* community and for general speculation regarding discontent among *conversos* as discrimination and persecution against them intensified. However, they offer a limited perspective for considering *converso* literature. Typologies of *conversos* do not take into account temporal and ideological differences among individuals, a limitation recognized by both Gitlitz (84–85) and Faur (43), and for this reason cannot be employed as the basis for literary interpretations. In literary analysis, typological assumptions might encourage preconceived readings which, while not necessarily erroneous, suggest that texts are solely motivated by particular religious beliefs (that is, an adherence to Judaism or Christianity) or reflect their author's desire to reach a specific public. Overdependence on such assumptions might lead to one of the pitfalls underscored by Paul Julian Smith: "the work of theory . . . is to account for the 'sense of self' felt by a minority or community without falling back into a naïve belief in the unchanging identity of that minority or community. Whatever the position adopted by the theorist, however, there can be no monolithic sense of the woman, the Jew, or the *converso* as homogenous entities, as always the same. They carry difference within them" (28). My search for the terms and phrases that delineate this "sense of self" reveals patterns of literary discourse that surface whether or not the authors in question suffered direct persecution and with an implicit acceptance of their undoubtedly varied ideologies.

The ideological heterogeneity of the *conversos* does not negate that certain works may be understood as *converso* texts. Nor is such an understanding contradicted by the historical heterogeneity of *converso* communities, a concept that must be taken into account when discussing the impact of discrimination, as David Nirenberg has established in his analysis of fourteenth-century Aragonese conflicts between Jews and Christians: "although the form and vocabulary of stereotypes about and accusations against minorities (poison, magic, sexuality, and so forth) may seem very similar across time and geographic space, their function and effect are closely dependent on social context and conflict, and therefore differ greatly from time to time and place to place" (124). Nirenberg's argument against teleological historicism lends support to my interpretation of the events that transpired in Spain during the late Middle Ages. As I demonstrate in the following chapter, persecution against *conversos*, while undoubtedly grounded in latent pan-European anti-Judaism, erupted in fifteenth-century Castile (and in other regions) as a result of different, and at times localized, political and economic factors. As the second half of the century progressed, there was a growing tendency for the consequences of this persecution to affect large sectors of the Castilian *converso* community. To be sure, much of the *converso* population was never forced to endure first-hand anti-*converso* persecution. However, even those who did not suffer directly undoubtedly experienced some degree of perturbation due to the nature of anti-*converso* sentiment, according to which *conversos* were collectively assigned an intrinsic Jewishness and identified as inferior Christians. Although crypto-Jews (*conversos* who practiced Judaism in secret) were in theory the targets of purity-of-blood statutes and the Inquisition, in practice both sincere and insincere *conversos* suffered discrimination and persecution, and no distinction was made during the violent attacks on *converso* communities. As anti-*converso* persecution became a national (Castilian) phenomenon, the sociological bond among *conversos* became the genealogical stigma imposed on them by the dominant Old Christian majority.

In this study I endeavor to demonstrate that the *converso* works to be considered (and in the case of Juan Poeta, those written about him by Old Christians) reflect the nature and magnitude of anti-*converso* persecution. The texts in question are *converso* texts (written by *conversos*, except for the few cases just mentioned) because they depict an awareness of the progressive marginalization of the *conversos*. Of course, as Colbert Nepaulsingh points out in his analysis of *La vida de Lazarillo de Tormes, El Abencerraje,* and *Los siete libros de la Diana* as *converso* texts, "*Converso* authors do not always create *converso* texts; they are capable of other styles of composition" (5). A basic premise of my book, one that I reiterate in subsequent chapters, is that such a duality must at times be recognized within *converso* works. In other words, the revelation of a work's *converso* significance does not deny that the same work may be considered in other contexts as well.

My assertion that literature reveals the condition of being an inferior Christian participates in the tradition of deciphering codified discourse practiced by scholars such as Faur and Nepaulsingh. However, in the formulation of my own approach I do not subscribe to Nepaulsingh's notion that *converso* texts may be "written in such a way that Christians would understand them one way, while Jews would read the same words and understand them in a totally different, sometimes opposite, way" (x). Although the terms and phrases that must be decodified in order to ascertain their *converso* meanings are more obscure in some works, reception of these meanings did not depend on a contemporary reader's religion, a point that I discuss in more detail in Chapter 2.

Like any method of literary interpretation, semiotics, the theoretical method for my approach, understands that meaning derives from situating a text in a particular context. The context that concerns me is the sociopolitical situation in Castile during the second half of the fifteenth century and its reflection in literature dealing with themes that recall the inferiority of the *conversos*. Although literary texts (poetry and prose) are the primary focus of my study, nonliterary works are also considered for their significant impacts on the ideologies of *converso* literary works or when they help to illuminate the literature in question.

The literary works upon which I focus do not, of course, represent the entire corpus of works composed by *conversos* in fifteenth-century Castile. However, they constitute more than a mere cross-section of that corpus. These works are unique for their social themes, which, as I demonstrate, tie them to particular historical moments. My analyses, which I conduct according to chronological divisions of these works, ultimately reveal terms that form part of an evolving code of Otherness. This code, which I call the "*converso* code," consistently alludes to the inferiority of the *conversos* in terms that depict the evolution of anti-*converso* discrimination and persecution.

Chapter 1 comprises an in-depth discussion of the historical origins and development of this situation. In Chapter 2, I concisely define the parameters of my semiotic theoretical model. Chapter 3 is dedicated to illustrating the effectiveness of this model by applying it to the corpus of poetry involving Juan Poeta. Chapter 4, the first of four chapters devoted to analyzing the *converso* code as a response to the historical evolution of anti-

converso persecution, explores the impact of early Castilian humanistic thought on *converso* poets of the literary circle of Alfonso Carrillo. These poets incorporated egalitarian ideals grounded in humanism into their works as a reaction to the intensification and nationalization of anti-*converso* persecution during the 1460s and early 1470s. In Chapter 5, I discuss the *converso* response to the creation of a seemingly tolerant atmosphere by Queen Isabel the Catholic. Composed during the first six years of her reign, which coincided with a decrease in tensions between Old and New Christians, this corpus of works is characterized by its laudatory treatment of the queen in the name of Christian unity. In *converso* poetry Isabel is portrayed as a divine figure capable of creating a harmonious society, an attitude that contrasts sharply with the deprecatory tone that some of the same *converso* writers had adopted in their treatment of her predecessor, King Enrique IV. Chapters 6 and 7 focus on works, which I call "*converso* laments," composed after the establishment of the Inquisition in 1480. In being allegories that veil their *converso* meanings, these texts reflect a fear of the arbitrary nature of inquisitional persecution and an awareness of the severity of the social decline caused by the efficacy by which the Inquisition operated. In Chapter 8, I conclude by comparing the different manifestations of the *converso* code in order to review the outstanding features of the evolution of this literary discourse, and I make tentative assessments regarding its impact on contemporary religious, social, and intellectual ideologies.

1

The *Conversos*

A Historical Overview

During the early centuries of the Common Era, Spanish Jews (later known as Sephardim) prospered economically as a tolerated and legal sect in the Roman province of Hispania.[1] After the establishment of Visigothic rule, forced conversions of the Jews began to occur in the seventh century during a surge in anti-Judaism.[2] These baptisms took place in spite of the fact that they contradicted Christian doctrine, which stressed that conversion should be accomplished through preaching, gradual assimilation, and peaceful means, and that a sincere convert should be considered no different from one who was Christian by birth. The Church even called upon Christians to act as model citizens, in the hope that their example would eventually convince both pagans and Jews to become good Christians. However, the obligation imposed upon Jews to accept baptism inevitably produced insincere converts, and many relapsed into Judaism after conversion.

In 633 the Fourth Council of Toledo responded to this situation by issuing a number of canons dealing with Jews who converted to Christianity.[3] While the principal aim of the Fourth Council was to ensure that those who had relapsed would become good Christians, the promulgation of these canons appears to reflect a general mistrust of converts, an attitude that also informs successive royal and ecclesiastical legislation. Subsequent decrees enacted by King Recceswinth (r. 649–72) limited the rights of both Jews and converts (Parkes 360–61). In 655 the Ninth Council of Toledo obligated converts "to spend in the actual presence of the bishops all Jewish and Christian feast days" (Parkes 361). Two of Recceswinth's successors, King Erwig (r. 680–87) and King Egica (r. 687–702), imposed further prohibitions. The former passed "a series of laws regulating the position of the Hebrew Christians in the general community" (Parkes

364), and the latter decreed that any Christian of non-Jewish ancestry could bring the sincerity of a conversion into question (Parkes 367).

After the Muslim invasion of the Iberian Peninsula in the eighth century, the situation for many Jews gradually improved. Over the course of the next few centuries, Sephardim who resided under Ibero-Muslim rule achieved a level of prominence in literary and scientific spheres that was unparalleled in other Judeo-European communities of the Middle Ages. This cultural Golden Age of the Sephardim reached its pinnacle in the tenth and eleventh centuries, when Andalusian poets such as Judah Halevi, Moses ibn Ezra, and Solomon ibn Gabirol flourished in an atmosphere of religious tolerance.

The military successes of advancing Christian armies, along with the dissolution of the caliphate of Córdoba, brought the Golden Age of Sephardic culture to a close by the middle of the twelfth century. The rise of Islamic fundamentalism, marked by the arrival to Spain of the Almoravids and the Almohads, also helped to end religious tolerance under Muslim rule. While both the Almoravids and the Almohads succeeded in reuniting the petty kingdoms (*taifas*) into which the caliphate of Córdoba had been divided, this political cohesion signified the advent of religious persecution. Once again, the Sephardim became the victims of pogroms and legal restrictions and were ordered to convert. As life became more restrictive for the Sephardim, they, along with many Christians who had also been required to adopt Islam, began to emigrate north to the increasingly powerful and more tolerant Christian kingdoms.

In late medieval Christian Spain, the Sephardim would never achieve the prominence of their Golden Age, although they would continue to survive and even prosper as the Reconquest progressed. Jews were frequently utilized by monarchs as inhabitants of newly acquired territories, and they often played significant roles in managing financial and administrative affairs.[4] While this symbiotic relationship often afforded royal protection, their association with the monarchy would also make the Jews scapegoats in the eyes of the Christian masses, who blamed them for periods of economic hardship. Indeed, this historical moment marked a turning point in the history of Spain's Jewish community. While the Jews had been able to endure Visigothic and Islamic persecution, they would not be able to withstand the surge in anti-Judaism that began during the twelfth century.

As Joshua Trachtenberg explains in his comprehensive study of medieval anti-Judaism, accusations that Jews were engaged in crimes against

Christianity or other illicit activities—dealings with the Antichrist, poisoning the Christian population, involvement in ritual killings, desecrating the host, and so forth—were launched throughout Europe with growing frequency during the late twelfth and early thirteenth centuries. It was also at this time when a belief in the birth of the Antichrist (which was thought to portend a Jewish invasion of Christianity) became widespread and when "the doctrine of transubstantiation [which] was ecclesiastically established at the Fourth Lateran Council in 1215 . . . seems to have precipitated the birth of the legend of Jewish profanation of the host" (Trachtenberg 109). The Fourth Lateran Council participated in the dissemination of anti-Judaism by ordering Jews to wear distinctive emblems and by instituting an episcopal Inquistion, an action followed by the establishment of a papal Inquisition in 1231. While these Inquisitions did not have any official jurisdiction over Jews, there were a number of cases in which Jews could be brought before the tribunal, a reflection, as Edward Peters posits (80), of the prevalence of contemporary anti-Judaism.

In thirteenth-century Castile, anti-Jewish rhetoric was propagated on different levels of society. For example, Gonzalo de Berceo's *Milagros de Nuestra Señora*, which contains a number of references that reveal that it was intended to be read aloud to Christian pilgrims passing by the author's monastery of San Millán de la Cogolla, helped to foment anti-Judaism among the populace. Of course, while it is impossible to know the extent to which Berceo's public held this rhetoric to be true, Berceo may have been motivated by a desire to include a fashionable contemporary theme. As E. Michael Gerli explains, the objective of "Mester de Clerecía" poets such as Berceo was to compose their works in order to "facilitar la comunicación y aumentar la identificación del oyente con el relato" (facilitate communication and increase the identification of the listener with the tale) (Berceo 17). As an extension of this objective, it would have been imperative that literary characters embody widely held values and beliefs.

The fact that Berceo's collection includes several episodes that are hostile toward Jews may attest to the popularity of this sentiment. Resentment of Jewish affluence is depicted in Miracle 23 ("El mercader fiado"), which underscores the greed of a rich Jewish usurer, the wealthiest person in Constantinople (st. 636ab). After receiving payment for a loan he has made to a devout Christian merchant, the usurer exhibits his cupidity by pretending that he has not received the money. Miracle 25 ("De cómo Teófilo fizo carta con el diablo de su ánima et después fue convertido e salvo") depicts a Jew as a practitioner of witchcraft ("savié encantamientos e muchos maleficios" [st. 767b]), and as a companion of the devil ("Belzebud lo guïava en todos sus oficios" [st. 767d]). Miracle 18 ("Cristo y los judíos de Toledo") presents a group of Jews who are found crucifying a wax figure of Christ in the home "del raví más onrado" (st. 427a). This final charge is also leveled in poem number 12 (in Walter Mettmann's anthology) of the *Cantigas de Santa Maria* ("Esta é como Santa Maria se queixou en Toledo eno dia de ssa festa de agosto, porque os judeus crucifigavan ũa omagen de cera, a semellança de seu fillo"). Similar types of accusations are found on other occasions in the *Cantigas*, a collection of poems dedicated to the Virgin Mary that was composed in part by King Alfonso X el Sabio of Castile (r. 1252–84).[5] The presence of these accusations in the *Cantigas* confirms that they also circulated among the higher orders of society.

Widespread acceptance of anti-Jewish invective often lent it a measure of legitimacy as "popular legends . . . were freely incorporated into the chronicles and accepted as indubitable fact" (Trachtenberg 63). Las Siete Partidas, a legal code written between 1256 and 1265 under the direction of King Alfonso X (and officially promulgated in 1348 by King Alfonso XI), is testimony of this transformation. In "Título 24" of the seventh "Partida" ("De los judíos"), hearsay concerning Jewish involvement in ritual murders and sacrilegious crimes is substantiated by the classification of these acts as ones that must be adjudicated before the king:

> Et porque oyemos decir que en algunos lugares los judíos ficieron et facen el día del viernes santo remembranza de la pasión de nuestro señor Jesucristo en manera de escarnio, furtando los niños et poniéndolos en la cruz, o faciendo imágines de cera et crucificándolas quando los niños non pueden haber, mandamos que si fama fuere daquí adelante que en algunt lugar de nuestro señorío tal cosa sea fecha, si se pudiere averiguar que todos aquellos que se acertaren en aquel fecho que sean presos, et recabdados et aduchos antel rey. (Alfonso X 3:670)

The diffusion of other sections of Las Siete Partidas may have contributed to the growth of late medieval anti-Judaism. While the legal code appears to promote tolerance by respecting the Jewish Sabbath (Alfonso X 3:672), and by advocating the preservation of synagogues, which Christians are prohibited from desecrating (Alfonso X 3:671), this tolerance is consistently accompanied by restrictions. For example, although Jews may maintain their synagogues, they may not make any improvements to them (Alfonso X 3:671). In addition, Jews are prohibited from having sexual relations with Christians, visiting Christian baths, possessing Christian servants, seeking Christian converts to Judaism, or holding any public office that empowers them over Christians (Alfonso X 3:670–71), and they are required to wear distinctive emblems:

> et mandamos que todos quantos judíos et judías vivieren en nuestro señorío, que trayan alguna señal cierta sobre las cabezas, que sea atal por que conoscan las gentes manifiestamente quál es judío o judía. Et si algunt judío non levase aquella señal, mandamos que peche por cada vegada que fuese fallado sin ella diez maravedís de oro: et si non hobiere de que los pechar, reciba diez azotes públicamente por ello. (Alfonso X 3:675)[6]

Some scholars argue that the promulgation of these prohibitions was grounded in a royal desire to protect the Jewish population. For example, Joseph O'Callaghan writes, "In the centuries of Muslim dominance, Christians and Jews were tolerated minorities, protected by the Islamic state, and within certain limits, free to practice their own religions and to be governed by their own laws. Once in the ascendancy, Christians followed a similar policy, officially protecting and tolerating . . . Jews" (96).[7] On a cultural level, this assessment of Alfonso's reign is certainly true. Jews played an integral role in the thirteenth-century Castilian renaissance as scientists and translators, helping to reacquaint Europe with Greco-Roman knowledge that had been lost during the Middle Ages in addition to introducing Western society to the writings of philosophers such as Averroes and Maimonides.[8] In political and economic spheres, Jews also made significant contributions as tax collectors and royal secretaries, as well as serving as physicians and advisors at the court of Alfonso X.[9] With regard to the tolerant nature of this cooperation, Dwayne Carpenter asserts that, "in spite of increasingly antipathetic attitudes and policies toward Spanish Jewry, Alfonso's general posture in this regard is one of relative leniency. This is evident not only in the Alfonsine legislation itself, but also in comparison with the Jewish policies pursued by other European monarchs of the time. Despite what we might perceive as patently restrictive attitudes toward Jews on the part of Alfonso, when viewed in historical perspective, his position is perhaps best characterized as one of restrained tolerance" (5).

The statutes of Alfonso X are, in many respects, more lenient than those decreed by other European monarchs of the period. For example, the Jews were actually expelled from England in 1290 by Edward I, and from France in 1306 by Philip the Fair. At the same time, the clear dichotomy between Christians and Jews that exists in Las Siete Partidas invites speculation as to the extent to which Alfonso X actually envisioned a place for Jews in his kingdom. His attempt to restrict their activities and segregate them from the Christian community apparently left a lasting imprint on social attitudes toward Jews, as subsequent legislation suggests. Additional laws were passed in Zamora in 1313, and in Toro in 1371, which, among other things, required Jews to display outward signs of identification and to live separately from Christians, and also prohibited them from holding public office and from collecting rent from Christians.[10]

In Las Siete Partidas, Alfonso X enables Jews who convert to Christianity to improve their social status. In contrast to Visigothic and Islamic legislation, which had compelled the Jews to convert, Alfonso advocates a more peaceful procedure for convincing them to adopt Christianity. According to Las Siete Partidas, Jews are to be converted by "buenos exemplos, et con los dichos de las santas escripturas e con falagos," and not by force, which contradicts divine will: "nuestro señor Dios non quiere nin ama servicio quel sea fecho por fuerza" (Alfonso X 3:672). Furthermore, those who convert are treated with honor and respect, afforded the same opportunities as other Christians, and are permitted to retain their property:

> Otrosí mandamos que después que algunos judíos se tornaren cristianos, que todos los del nuestro señorío los honren: et ninguno non sea osado de retraer a ellos nin a su linage de como fueron judíos en manera de denuesto: et que hayan sus bienes et sus cosas ... et que puedan haber todos los oficios et las honras que han los otros cristianos. (Alfonso X 3:673)

This egalitarian attitude toward converts is reiterated further on in Las Siete Partidas:

> todos los cristianos et cristianas de nuestro señorío fagan honra et bien en todas las maneras que pudieren a todos aquellos que de las creencias extrañas vinieren a la nuestra fe, bien así como farién a otro qualquier que su padre, et su madre, et sus abuelos et sus abuelas hobiesen seído cristianos. (Alfonso X 3:677)

The king's plan to peacefully convert his Jewish subjects may be understood as a component of his nationalistic aims. The composition of Las

Siete Partidas represented an attempt to create political harmony through the imposition of a uniform set of laws. As an extension of this national- ism, the king's treatment of the Jews may indicate his desire to achieve this harmony through religious unity. In attempting to create an atmosphere conducive to conversion, Alfonso X may have taken his cue from the con- temporary European surge in systematic attempts to convert the Jews. A reform movement initiated by the Fourth Lateran Council led to an inten- sified effort to attract converts, an effort fomented by the proselytizing of the Dominicans and the Franciscans,[11] two preaching orders founded in the year 1216.

The prevalence of references to conversions in the *Milagros de Nuestra Señora* and the *Cantigas de Santa Maria* appears to reflect the zeal with which proselytizing was undertaken. In the aforementioned Miracle 23 ("El mercader fiado"), Berceo writes of a group of Jews ("elli con sus compannas") who convert after witnessing a supernatural event:

Fabló el crucifixo, díxoli buen mandado:
"Miente, ca paga priso en el día tajado;
el cesto en que vino el aver bien contado,
so el so lecho misme lo tiene condesado."

Movióse el pueblo todo como estava plecho,
fuéronli a la casa, fizieron grand derecho;
trovaron el escrinno do yazié so el lecho,
fincó el trufán malo confuso e maltrecho.

Si'l pesó o si'l plogo, triste e desmedrido,
ovo del pleito todo a venir connocido,
elli con sus compannas fo luego convertido,
murió enna fe buena, de la mala tollido. (st. 694–96abcd)

In Miracle 16 ("El judezno"), Berceo relates the tale of a Jewish boy who, while participating in an Easter mass, is enchanted by the benevo- lence and beauty of an effigy of the Virgin:

Mientre que comulgavan a muy grand presura
el ninno judezno alzó la catadura,
vío sobre'l altar una bella figura,
una fermosa duenna con genta creatura.

Vío que esta duenna que posada estava,
a grandes e a chicos ella los comulgava;

pagóse d'ella mucho, quando más la catava
de la su fermosura más se enamorava. (st. 357–58abcd)

The boy then takes Communion (which represents his conversion to
Christianity), an act that he reveals to his father upon returning home.
After hearing what his son has done, the boy's father proceeds to throw
him into an oven. However, the boy is not harmed because he is protected
by an apparition of the Virgin (an event that further symbolizes his conversion), as he relates to the Jews and Christians who have gathered in
amazement:

Preguntáronli todos, judíos e christianos
cómo podió venzer fuegos tan sobranzanos,
quando él non mandava los piedes ni las manos
quí lo cabtenié entro, fiziésselos certanos.

Recudiólis el ninno palavra sennalada:
"La duenna que estava enna siella orada
con su fijo en brazos sobre'l altar posada,
éssa me defendié que non sintié nada."

Entendieron que era Sancta María ésta,
que lo defendió ella de tan fiera tempesta;
cantaron grandes laudes, fizieron rica festa,
metieron esti miraclo entre la otra gesta. (st. 368–70abcd)

As a result of his attempt to kill his son, the boy's father is himself cast into
a fire in Berceo's work, a punishment that parallels the severe penalty
Alfonso X imposes in Las Siete Partidas upon Jews who persecute Jewish
converts to Christianity:

Otrosí decimos que si algunt judío o judía de su grado se quisiere
tornar cristiano o cristiana, non gelo deben embargar nin defender los
otros judíos en ninguna manera; et si alguno dellos lo apedreasen, o lo
firiesen o lo matasen porque se quisiese facer cristiano o después que
fuese baptizado, si esto se pudiese probar o averiguar, mandamos que
todos los matadores et los consejadores de tal muerte o apedrea-
miento sean quemados. (3:672–73)

Five *Cantigas* (in Mettmann's anthology, numbers 4, 25, 85, 89, and
107) also voice the promise of a brighter future for Jews who accept Christianity. In *Cantiga* 4 ("Ésta é como Santa Maria guardou ao fillo do judeu
que non ardesse, que seu padre deitara no forno"), a version of the tale that

Berceo includes as Miracle 16 ("El judezno"), the Jewish boy's official conversion to Christianity is underscored by the explicit mention of his baptism: "o batismo recebia" (Mettmann 66). *Cantiga* 85 ("Como Santa Maria livrou de morte un judeu que tiinnan preso hũus ladrões, e ela soltó-o da prijon, e feze-o tornar crischão"), describes how the Virgin helps a Jew to escape persecution by guiding him toward conversion:

> Que mais de çen mil maneiras as almas peavan
> dos judeus, que as cozian e pois ar assavan
> e as fazian arder assi como tições,
> e queimando-lle-las barvas e pois os grinões.
> > Pera toller gran perfia
> > > ben dos corações,
> > demostra Santa Maria
> > > sas grandes visiões.
> Quand' o judeu viu aquesto, foi end' espantado;
> mais tan toste foi a outro gran monte levado
> u viu seer Jesu-Cristo con religiões
> d' angeos, que sempre cantan ant' el doçes sões.
> > Pera toller gran perfia
>
> . . . .
> Santa Maria lle disse, pois est' ouve visto:
> "Estes son meus e de meu Fillo, Deus Jesu-Cristo,
> con que serás se creveres en el e leytões
> comeres e leixares a degolar cabrões."
> > Pera toller gran perfia
>
> . . . .
> Pois que Santa Maria lle diss' este fazfeiro,
> leixó-o: e el foi-sse log' a un mõesteiro
> u achou un sant' abade con seus conpannões,
> que partiron mui de grado con el sas rações. (Mettmann 270)

Attempts to convert the Spanish Jews during the 1200s met with little success. But by the end of the following century, relations between Jews and Christians would deteriorate to the point that thousands of Jews were forced to convert in order to save their lives and property. The latent medieval anti-Judaism present in the aforementioned beliefs concerning Jewish involvement in illicit activities cannot be considered the sole cause for this calamity. The fourteenth-century intensification of anti-Judaism can be attributed to nonreligious factors as well, and it parallels a growing intolerance of other minorities. For example, as Nirenberg demonstrates, accusations of well poisoning in Aragón in 1321 targeted lepers and Muslims in addition to Jews, and charges were leveled because of political motives rather than general religious scapegoating (93–124). Nirenberg's argument against the eschatological and essentialist explanations for the demise of the medieval Spanish Jewish community offered by historians such as Baer sheds new light on the origins of that demise in northeastern Spain and encourages examinations of regional circumstances. At the same time, when considered together, the well-poisoning scare of 1321, the Aragonese Shepherd's Crusade of 1320 (also discussed by Nirenberg [69–92]), outbreaks of the Black Plague (beginning in 1348),[12] and political and economic crises reflect a fourteenth-century increase in events that victimized the Jews. The collective nature of this intensified anti-Judaism is found in the consequences rather than the causes. In other words, latent anti-Judaism was brought to the surface in fourteenth-century Spain through a series of cataclysmic events that differed from region to region but that collectively focused attention on Jews and inspired anti-Jewish hostility. While the causes for this increased animosity varied, the ultimate consequences (the pogroms of 1391) reverberated throughout Spain in the conversion of multitudes of Jews.

In Castile a struggling economy and political turmoil, in addition to the arrival of the Black Plague, laid the foundation for 1391. Because of the close ties of Jewish financial officials to the monarchy, Jews were held responsible for a severe economic crisis in Castile—actually the result of a weak infrastructure[13]—and were associated with the despised figure of the tax collector who took advantage of the common people. This resentment resonates in Pero López de Ayala's late fourteenth-century work, "Rimado de palacio":

> Sobre los ynoçentes cuytados pecadores:
> Luego que han acordado llaman arrendadores.
>   Allí vienen judíos, que están aparejados
> Para vever la sangre de los pobres cuytados:
> Presentan sus escriptos que tienen conçertados,
> E prometen sus joyas e dones apriuados.
>   Perlados que sus eglesias deuían gouernar,
> Por cobdiçia del mundo allí quieren morar,
> E ayudan reuoluer el regno a más andar,
> Cómo rebueluen tordos vn pobre palomar.
>   Allí fasen judíos el su repartimiento

Sobre el pueblo que muere por mal defendimiento,
E ellos entre sy apartan luego medio cuento
Que han de auer priuados, qual ochenta, qual çiento. (432–33)

The declaration by King Enrique II (r. 1369–79), in 1367, that Jews were the only ones willing to be tax collectors (Castro, *The Structure* 499),[14] suggests that, rather than the bias of a particular individual, López de Ayala's literary vision reflected popular animosity toward Jewish economic influence. This animosity undoubtedly led to the Jews' becoming economic scapegoats during the civil war between Enrique and his half-brother, King Pedro I (r. 1350–69).[15] In 1355 the Jews of Toledo, in part because of their wealth, were the victims of a violent attack, as López de Ayala relates in his chronicle of the events:

E el Conde [Enrique] é el Maestre, desque entraron en la cibdad, asosegaron en sus posadas; pero las sus compañas comenzaron á robar una judería apartada que dicen el Alcana, é robaronla, é mataron los Judíos que fallaron fasta mil é docientas personas, omes é mugeres, grandes é pequeños. (*Crónica del rey don Pedro* 462)

In reaction to this assault, King Pedro, whose government included many Jews in economic posts, chose to defend the Jewish community:

E traía el Rey muchas gentes consigo. . . . Pasaron fasta trecientos omes de armas, ayudandoles los Judíos que en la judería estaban con cuerdas de cañamo que les daban, é pasaban el río por las azudas teniendose á las cuerdas. E estos que así pasaron entraron en la judería mayor, é juntaronse con los que estaban en el castillo de la judería, que tenían la parte del Rey Don Pedro, é defendieron la judería. (López de Ayala, *Crónica del rey don Pedro* 462–63)

As the conflict progressed, the Jews became increasingly identified with the oppressive reign of King Pedro, and Enrique's anti-Jewish posture, including his participation in the murder of the Jews of Nájera in 1360, was instrumental in divesting Pedro of public support:

El Rey Don Pedro estando en Burgos sopo como el Conde Don Enrique, é Don Tello, é el Conde de Osona, é los otros Caballeros que con ellos venían, eran ya entrados en Castilla, é como llegaron á Nájera, é ficieron matar á los Judíos. E esta muerte de los Judíos fizo fazer el Conde Don Enrique, porque las gentes lo facían de buena voluntad, é por el fecho mesmo tomaban miedo é recelo del Rey

[Pedro], é tenían con el Conde. (López de Ayala, *Crónica del rey don Pedro* 503)

Enrique's supporters proclaimed him king of Castile in 1366. As his victory over Pedro drew close, he further enhanced his image by inflicting punishment on the Jews of Toledo, whom he obligated to provision his assemblage:

> el Rey Don Enrique entró en Toledo, é todos le rescibieron con grand placer, é con grandes alegrías, é estovo allí quince días pagando sus gentes: é estonce el Aljama de los Judíos de Toledo le sirvió para pagar las Compañas que venían con él. (López de Ayala, *Crónica del rey don Pedro* 542)

After his victory, Enrique appeared to change his position, and he, like his predecessor, employed Jews as financial officials. However, even after the king altered his policy, little could be done to stem the growing tide of popular anti-Jewish sentiment.

In 1391 the situation reached its flash point. The fervent anti-Jewish sermons of the archdeacon of Écija, Ferrand Martínez, inspired the Christian masses to attack the Jews. Many Jews were killed in Sevilla, where the violence first erupted, and in a number of other cities such as Burgos, Córdoba, and Toledo.[16] Although Martínez's sermons provoked the outbreak of violence, the Christians were also motivated to strike for economic reasons. A period of high inflation during the years immediately prior to 1391 had made life difficult for all Castilians, who targeted the Jews in order to vent their frustration at the royal policy of debasing the coinage in order to fund foreign wars (MacKay, "Popular Movements" 54).

In the wake of this violence thousands of Jews were compelled to convert to Christianity. After another period of inflation between 1412 and 1416 caused by an agricultural crisis (MacKay, "Popular Movements" 56–57), thousands more became Christians. The proselytizing of Vicente Ferrer, a Dominican friar, and the efforts of two *conversos*, Pablo de Santa María and Jerónimo de Santa Fe, also contributed to this second wave of conversions.

Benzion Netanyahu believes that as many as 400,000 conversions occurred between 1391 and 1416 and that there were some 650,000 *conversos* in Spain by around 1480 (*The Marranos* 235–45). More recently, Norman Roth has speculated that there may have been as many as 750,000 *conversos* in Spain during the late fifteenth century (332). However, a number of scholars consider these estimates to be inflated, and the more accepted opinion is that there were only around 225,000 *conversos* by this time (Gitlitz 74). In any case, the number of conversions that took place was unprecedented in Spain. In a span of a little more than twenty years, many long-standing centers of Judaism were transformed into communities of *conversos*. During the following three decades some of these *conversos* succeeded in bureaucratic professions that were traditionally occupied by Jews.

Although it was not until "the reign of Enrique IV that conversos rose to prominent posts in the largest numbers" (Roth 120), *conversos* were already successful in government service during the reign of Juan II due to the nature of contemporary Spanish society, which "was characterised by a pronounced demand for technicians in economic and bureaucratic activity" (Márquez Villanueva, "The Converso Problem" 318). Examples included Pedro de la Caballería, a renowned jurist, Fernán Díaz de Toledo, a royal secretary, Lope Fernández Cota, a royal scribe, and many more on the municipal level. Other *conversos* rose through the ecclesiastical ranks, such as Pablo de Santa María and his son, Alonso de Cartagena, who both became bishops of Burgos, and Jerónimo de Santa Fe, who became the pope's personal physician. At the other end of the spectrum, many *conversos* during the early 1400s were the victims of grassroots discrimination, which restricted their chances for social advancement, as Netanyahu notes: "most converts were destitute when they entered Christendom. . . . The only chance for the converts to get work . . . was to turn to the Christian burghers; but the Christians, who would generally not engage Jews unless moved by some special reason to do so, maintained the same attitude toward the converts" (*The Origins* 207–8).

Discrimination against these first generations of *conversos* was not only directed at those who could not escape the lower economic strata. Márquez Villanueva asserts that by the early 1420s the monopolization by *conversos* of the bureaucracy had "started to irritate the [Old Christian] proletarian masses" ("The Converso Problem" 318).[17] Contemporary literature provides evidence of such animosity toward *conversos* in the bureaucracy, as Francisca Vendrell Gallostra explains in her analysis of two poems that Juan de Dueñas dedicated to King Juan II (r. 1406–54). For example, in "Coplas . . . al sennor Rey de Castilla" Dueñas begrudges the success of the *conversos* at court while Old Christians are suffering:

Y por esto, sennor fuerte,
no deurías consentir
a los tales reçebir

merced ni bienes en suerte,
quanto más a los conversos,
de los buenos más adversos
que la vida de la muerte. (Vendrell Gallostra 110)

As Scholberg establishes, this same attitude is evident in a poem ("Coplas sobre la gala")[18] by another Old Christian, Suero de Ribera, who, like Dueñas, depicts "los rencores que sentían los cristianos viejos contra los burócratas conversos de la cancillería real" (the rancor that Old Christians felt toward *converso* bureaucrats of the royal chancellery) (349).

This discriminatory attitude persisted despite marriage by *conversos* into Old Christian families. In the "Instrucción del relator" (published in 1449), Fernán Díaz de Toledo, a New Christian himself, observed that *conversos* throughout Spain had mixed into families from many levels of society—including the nobility, the clergy, and the middle class—and that it was difficult to ascertain exactly who possessed a Jewish lineage:

> todos los Judíos de España . . . de los que de estos descienden, quién sabe quáles son. E en nuestros tiempos fue el Revendo Padre Don Pablo, Obyspo de Burgos, de buena memoria e Canciller mayor de el Rey, e de su Consejo; e sus nietos e viznietos, e sobrinos, e los otros de su Linage son ya oy en los Linages de los Manriques, e Mendosas e Roxas, e Saravias e Pestines. [*sic*] e Luyanes e Solys, e Mirandas, e Ossorios, e Salcedos, o otros Linages, e Solares, e algunos de ellos son viznietos de Juan Furtado de Mendoza, Mayordomo mayor de el Rey, y de el Maryscal Diego Fernández de Córdoba, sobrino de los mayores de el Reyno. E assí mesmo Juan de Sánchez de Sevilla, que era de este Linage, e era Contador mayor de el Rey, sus nietos y trasviznietos son hoy los de Araujo, e los de Porrás, e los de Valdéz, e de Anaya, e de Ocampo, e de Monroy, e de Solis de Sosa, e de Villaquirán, e los de Bobadilla, e de otros linages. Y mucho menos habrá mejoría de los que habrá de aquí a cien años. Y que cuidado tiene Juan Manuel de Olanda, porque es nieto de Francisco Fernández Marmolejo, Contador mayor de el Rey N.S. que fue, el que venía de este Linage, de el qual esto mesmo están hoy en Sevilla muchos regidores e caballeros, e oficiales de ella. Ca ansí mesmo los Nietos e Viz-nietos de Diego Sánchez de Valladolid, Contador mayor de el Rey, e de sus quentas. Los unos son de Santi-Esteban, e los otros de Motiçón e Bernáldes, los otros de otros linages e solares, e los nietos de mi primo e Señor Alfonso Álbares, eso mesmo algunos de ellos son de San-

dobal, e de los Carrillos, e de los Cerbantes, e otros de Alarcón, e otros de Viello, e ansí de otros Linages e solares. E los nietos de el Dr. Fonico: los unos son de Abellaneda, e los dos otros de Cuellar, e los de Peña Loza; e algunos de mis nietos de Barrionuevo, e Soto-Mayor, e Mendosa, e descienden de Juan Hurtado de Mendosa, el Viejo, Mayordomo mayor, de el Rey, que era un traviz-abuelo: y assí podía henchir papel de otros muchos. . . . hay muchos Linages en Castilla, fijos, e Nietos e Vis-nietos de el linage de Israel, ansi legos, como Clerigos, ansi de el linage de Nobles, como de caballeros, e Ciudadanos. . . . y hay semejantes en Aragón, e en otras partes. (351–55)

Discrimination continued in spite of these intermarriages, as the "Instrucción" illustrates:

que los que están fuera de la Fee, mayormente los Judíos, se han de convidar y atraer a ella por alagos, e ruegos, e beneficios, e por otras maneras de buena, e graciosa enceñanza para los ganar a fabor hijos de Dios, e que los Christianos los deben ayudar, y socorrer y honrar, y tratar fraternalmente y caritativamente y aun con todo amor, sin hacer departimiento, no distinción alguna de los antiguos a los nuevos, antes en algunas cosas los deben faborecer e facer ventaja, más que a otros, hasta que sean plantados, e radicados en la Santa Fee, según se face a los novicios en la religión. . . . Nin puedo entender que por algunos se convertir, e tornar Christiano, por eso ha errado nin fecho pecado alguno por que tan grande pena, e injuria, e ofensa de Dios, y en contumelia de esta Santa Fee, deba padecer, mayormente que la Sacra Escritura, dice en diversos lugares (como su merced sabe) que todos honren a los que vienen a la Ley, y los traten como hermanos, y les den parte y heredamiento en la tierra, y en todas las otras cosas, ansí como los mysmos, como de la propia Ley. (347–50)

While *conversos* may have joined the professional ranks and married into Old Christian families, Díaz de Toledo's admonition that a distinction should not be made between old and new members of the faith testifies to the undercurrents of anti-*converso* sentiment stirring among Old Christians.

The "Instrucción" was one of several treatises composed by *conversos* in response to the Toledo rebellion of 1449, an event that culminated in the first legal distinction between Old and New Christians. Although this rebellion was inspired by an economic crisis for which the *conversos* were not responsible,[19] they were attacked because they were associated with financial oppression. The event also brought to light the bias toward *conversos* held by Old Christians. Because they possessed Jewish ancestries, the *conversos* of Toledo were considered to be heretical Christians, and were treated by the Old Christians of Toledo as a collective enemy. This classification of the *conversos* as inferior Christians, which was expressed during the Toledo rebellion in the first *estatuto de limpieza de sangre* (purity-of-blood statute), would be repeated time and time again in statutes issued in other cities, in military and religious orders, and in universities.

The rebellion began when the Old Christians attacked Alonso Cota, a *converso* municipal treasurer and a "mercader muy rico" (Pérez de Guzmán 661, 663), who had been ordered by the royal *condestable*, Álvaro de Luna, to collect a tax from the citizens of Toledo. Because of Cota's diligence—and probably in part because of the animosity his wealth inspired—the Old Christians, under the leadership of Pero Sarmiento, an *alcalde mayor*, revolted against Luna and King Juan II by taking control of the city in order to protest the collection of the tax. At its core, the rebellion of 1449 was grounded in a belief by the citizens of Toledo that they were exempt from paying such royal taxes (Benito Ruano, *Toledo* 34–35). However, the involvement of Cota in the collection of the tax brought popular anti-*converso* sentiment to the fore and resulted in grave consequences for the *conversos* that extended well beyond the local level.

Shortly after the insurrection commenced, the social designs of Sarmiento's forces became evident. Cota and the rest of the *converso* population of Toledo were treated by the Old Christians as visible representatives of royal tyranny, and they were unjustly blamed for impoverishing the community.[20] Henceforth, the rebellion concentrated on the New Christians. Although royal authorities eventually regained control of the city, the *conversos* were victimized by the promulgation by Sarmiento's band of the Sentencia-Estatuto. This edict, the first purity-of-blood statute, expelled the *conversos* from service in civil and ecclesiastical office in Toledo and deemed them ineligible for future service in such positions (or as judicial witnesses) because their Christianity was tainted by their Jewish heritage:

> que todos los dichos conversos descendientes del perverso linaje de los judíos . . . como por razón de las herejías e otros delictos . . . sean habidos . . . por infames, inhábiles, incapaces e indignos para haber todo oficio e beneficio público y privado . . . incapaces para dar testimonio e fe como escribanos públicos o como testigos . . . que sean

privados de qualesquier oficios e beneficios que han habido e tienen.
(Benito Ruano, *Toledo* 194–95)[21]

The legacy of the Sentencia-Estatuto and its systematic legal discrimination against the *conversos* spread as additional purity-of-blood statutes were issued in the Fuero de Vizcaya (1452), Bilbao (1463), Ciudad Real (1468), Córdoba (1473), Guipúzcoa (1482), the Colegio de Santa Cruz in Valladolid (1488), the Orden de San Jerónimo (1493), and the Monasterio de Santo Tomás de Aquino de Ávila (1496).[22]

It must be noted that purity-of-blood statutes were not always enforced. The promulgation of the Sentencia-Estatuto, for example, did not prevent *conversos* from returning to public office during the 1450s and 1460s, a fact confirmed by the repeated expulsion in 1468 (by Enrique IV) of *conversos* from the municipal government of Toledo. Some *conversos* also employed fraud and perjury in order to secure entrance into organizations that had restricted them (Kamen, *The Spanish Inquisition: A Historical Revision* 242). At the same time, the need to go to such lengths attests to the effectiveness of the purity-of-blood statutes as weapons of intimidation. Their existence proclaimed the inferiority of the *conversos* and forced them to conceal their ancestry. One example may have been Gonzalo Fernández de Oviedo y Valdés (1478–1557), who served as a page to the Catholic Monarchs and as *secretario* of the Consejo de la Suprema Inquisición. Although Oviedo y Valdés was an "hombre de tan monstruosa memoria y proclive al nimio chisme biográfico" (a man with such an enormous memory and an awareness of the smallest biographical details) (Alcalá and Sanz 59), he conspicuously left out information regarding his forbears in the autobiographical sections of his works. According to Ángel Alcalá:

nada dijo de sus padres, por lo que se ha pensado que esos apellidos si no necesariamente falseados bajo la capa de origen asturiano acreedor a rancios linages, pueden ocultar ascendencia judeoconversa que el escrito discretamente prefirió silenciar. (Alcalá and Sanz 59)

[he said nothing about his parents, because of which it has been thought that those surnames (Oviedo and Valdés), perhaps falsified in order to give the appearance of an ancient (pure Christian) Asturian lineage, could hide a Jewish ancestry that is discreetly left unspoken in his works.]

The omission of a tainted family name in public declarations and official records was a precaution that was taken at considerable risk. Those who unsuccessfully attempted to circumvent the statutes could face dangerous consequences:

> If pretendants to office could not offer convincing genealogical proofs, comisarios were appointed to visit the localities concerned and take sworn statements from witnesses about the antecedents of the applicant.... In an age when written evidence was rare, the reputation of applicants lay wholly at the mercy of local gossip and hostile neighbours. Bribery became necessary. If an applicant was refused a post with the Inquisition the tribunal never gave any reason, with the result that the family of the man became suspected of impurity even if this was not the case.... Frequently applicants would be disabled from employment simply by the malicious gossip of enemies, because 'common rumour' was allowed as evidence. (Kamen, *The Spanish Inquisition: A Historical Revision* 242)

An additional consequence of the insurrection of 1449 was the deterioration of the relationship between the *conversos* and the Castilian monarchy. During the early 1400s, *conversos* were able to prosper in the bureaucracy due to the relative stability of the government. Juan II's immediate reaction to the promulgation of the Sentencia-Estatuto indicates that he desired to maintain this symbiosis. The king did not hesitate in petitioning Pope Nicholas V for the excommunication of Sarmiento and for a condemnation of the Sentencia-Estatuto. Several months later the pope issued the requested bull, in which all discrimination against *conversos* was also reproved (Benito Ruano, *Toledo* 53). During the next two years the king continued his campaign against the Sentencia-Estatuto, and in 1451, with papal consent, he confiscated the property of the perpetrators of the rebellion and sentenced them to death.[23]

This pro-*converso* attitude would quickly fade, however, because of the political significance of the Toledo rebellion. The event posed a serious threat to royal sovereignty because the perpetrators had refused to pay a royal tax, prohibited the king from entering Toledo, and defied his authority by aligning themselves with the prince. The Sentencia-Estatuto also usurped the king's control over public officials by legitimizing the expulsion of the *conversos*. As time progressed, it became increasingly apparent that the monarchy could not continue to maintain control over its citizenry and oppose Sarmiento's statute, the doctrines of which were rapidly disseminated in texts composed in support of Sarmiento's actions. In one treatise known as the "Memorial" (1449), Marcos García de Mora attempted to justify the Sentencia-Estatuto on the grounds that discrimination against *conversos* was grounded in canon law. Another, the anonymous "Traslado de una carta de privilegio que el rey Don Juan II dio a un hidalgo" (c. 1450), was "escrito como propaganda en favor de la acción de los cristianos viejos . . . [y en] contra [d]el Rey por su política favorable a los advenedizos" (written as propaganda in support of the actions of the Old Christians . . . [and] against the king for his favorable policies toward those upstarts) (Scholberg 349–51).

Royal protection of the *conversos* would eventually be sacrificed in order to prevent the outbreak of insurrections similar in nature to the Toledo rebellion. Such an event had already occurred in Ciudad Real, only two weeks after the promulgation of the Sentencia-Estatuto, when a group of Old Christians again challenged royal authority by attacking the *conversos* and expelling them from public office (Benito Ruano, *Toledo* 49–50). In 1451, the same year in which he had punished the Old Christians who had participated in the Toledo insurrection, Juan II acquiesced to public opinion by pardoning the followers of Sarmiento and sanctioning the provisions of the Sentencia-Estatuto.[24] At the king's request, the pope altered his position toward Sarmiento's band by issuing bulls in 1450 and 1451 that suspended the penalty of excommunication that he had previously imposed.[25]

The political, economic, and agricultural instability that characterized the last years of Juan II's reign were to evolve into a "severe and prolonged crisis" in the years 1465–73, during the reign of his son, Enrique IV (r. 1454–74) (MacKay, "Popular Movements" 57). The situation degenerated even further when increased tensions between the king and the nobility succeeded in destabilizing the Castilian monarchy. The climax occurred in 1464 with the eruption of a civil war, during which Enrique IV was symbolically deposed by the nobility (in 1465), who aligned themselves with the king's half-brother, Alfonso (who died in 1468).[26] Although all Castilians were forced to live through a difficult period, the crisis was especially difficult for the *conversos*, who were blamed for the struggling economy.[27]

The general scapegoating of the *conversos* for the economic downturn of Castile produced repeated attacks on them during the 1460s. Although political and economic factors contributed to the inceptions of these popular insurrections, as in 1449 they quickly became religiously motivated and the *conversos* became the primary victims. One of the worst outbreaks occurred in Toledo in 1467, when the *conversos* were once again attacked for their role in the collection of funds. This time, as a result of a dispute concerning rent payments, the Old Christians killed several *conversos* in addition to razing their neighborhoods.[28] During Enrique IV's reign, however, violence was not restricted to Toledo; in the 1460s and early 1470s, anti-*converso* riots occurred on a regular basis: in Carmona (1462), Toledo, Sevilla, and Burgos (1467), Sepúlveda (1471), Córdoba, Montoro, and many other towns in Andalucía (1473), and in Carmona, Segovia, Valladolid, and elsewhere (1474).

Prior to 1460, no organized national movement supported localized anti-*converso* sentiment. Alonso de Espina, a Franciscan monk and royal confessor to Enrique IV, formulated the agenda for such a movement in the *Fortalitium fidei contra Judaeos* (1460).[29] Espina's book reflected the pressure being placed upon the monarchy by high-ranking members of the Church who advocated a purification of the Christian faith. This purge necessitated the exclusion of Christians who were traditionally associated with heresy along with other enemies of the faith, namely, the *conversos* and the Jews. To this end Espina evoked many anti-*converso* and anti-Jewish libels in the course of elaborating a plan that foreshadowed the events of the following decades: the *conversos* were to be subject to an Inquisition in order to weed out the heretics, and the Jews were to be expelled from Spain. Espina's anti-*converso* rhetoric in a work that was widely disseminated gave added incentive to an already suspicious and volatile populace. As Henry Lea asserts, to Espina "may be ascribed a large share in hastening the development of organized persecution in Spain" (1:148–49). King Enrique IV did not delay in responding to the *Fortalitium:* in 1461 he issued a request to Pope Pius II for the establishment of a Castilian Inquisition.[30] Although the king failed to act on the papal bull he received, he did sanction a nonpapal episcopal Inquisition during the 1460s.[31]

Enrique IV's tergiversation and a decline in his political authority expedited the transformation of widespread anti-*converso* sentiment into recurring attacks. Although during the early years of his reign "we have no indication that Enrique's administration would permit anti-Marrano disturbances or allow them to pass with impunity" (Netanyahu, *The Origins* 716), the king adopted an anti-*converso* posture during his latter years on the throne. In addition to sanctioning an Inquisition, in 1468, after the social unrest in Toledo, he ratified the provisions of Sarmiento's Sentencia-Estatuto and "conceded to the city of Ciudad Real the privilege of excluding *conversos* from all municipal office" (Kamen, *The Spanish Inquisition*

32). Enrique IV also pardoned the Old Christians who participated in anti-*converso* uprisings during the 1460s and failed to punish the perpetrators of the Andalusian pogroms of the early 1470s (Netanyahu, *The Origins* 812). These actions and his inability to create a strong central government left the *conversos* unprotected. Consequently, anti-*converso* persecution became a national phenomenon.

When Enrique IV's reign came to an end in 1474, Old and New Christians looked toward a new monarchy with messianic expectations. Public perception was grounded in the hope that the ascension to the throne of Queen Isabel of Castile (r. 1474–1504) and King Fernando of Aragón (r. 1479–1516) might bring political stability and an end to social conflicts. According to Castro, "a fines del siglo XV las masas españolas creyeron que los Reyes Católicos habían sido enviados por Dios para instaurar la felicidad sobre la tierra, y para concluir con la tiranía de todos los poderosos" (toward the end of the fifteenth century the Spanish masses believed that the Catholic Monarchs had been sent by God in order to establish happiness and end tyranny throughout the land) (*La realidad* 242). In Castile the change of power had special implications for *conversos* and Jews. Unlike her predecessor, Isabel appeared to support the interests of her Jewish subjects on several occasions. During the late 1470s she (with Fernando's support) abolished restrictions that had been placed on Jews in Medina de Pomar, Sevilla, and Cáceres (Rubin 178). In 1477 Isabel also asserted, "All Jews in my realm . . . are mine and under my care and my protection and it belongs to me to defend and aid them and keep justice" (Sachar 63).[32]

Although this protective attitude reflected Isabel's conviction that the Jews were an important economic resource, it was undoubtedly seen by *conversos* as an indication of greater tolerance (at least by the monarchy) toward both the Jews and themselves. The queen personally attempted to improve relations between Old and New Christians by "order[ing] a public campaign of religious education" (Rubin 186) in order to instruct *conversos* in Christian doctrine. In addition, she maintained a hesitant attitude from 1478 until 1480 toward enforcing the bull (issued by Pope Sixtus IV) that authorized a Spanish Inquisition that would be controlled by the monarchy. The fact that after 1474 there were no more anti-*converso* uprisings appeared to signify that her policies would result in more amicable relations between Old and New Christians on the local level.

Any optimism created during this brief window was curtailed during the early 1480s, when inquisitorial tribunals officially began to operate.

The advent of the Holy Office affirmed that popular anti-*converso* sentiment had gained royal support and that all *conversos* would continue to
live in fear of both physical and legal persecution. Although the institution
was brought into existence in order to seek out and punish true heretics,
the prevalence of anti-*converso* sentiment and the existence of purity-of-
blood statutes helped to create an atmosphere in which all *conversos* were
at risk. Cases based on false accusations were not uncommon, and any
number of minor infractions, including practices that may have been followed out of habit by *conversos* who were not crypto-Jews, aroused suspicion:

> Lo que sí puede afirmarse es que no todos los condenados como judíos
> por la Inquisición lo eran realmente, pues a los ojos de los inqui-
> sidores eran indicios de judaísmo prácticas, hábitos y costumbres que
> ni aun la conversión más sincera podía desarraigar, como la aversión
> al cerdo, convertida en hábito fisiológico que no podía vencerse con
> argumentos teológicos. . . . [S]ería desacierto notable medir esta cor-
> riente [criptojudaísmo] a través de los procesos inquisitoriales, pues
> cuanto más se estudian éstos, mayores se van haciendo las dudas de
> que todos los condenados fueran apóstatas con el mínimo de con-
> ciencia culpable que permitiera considerarlos como auténticos judai-
> zantes. Los inquisidores consideraban prueba de apostasía la práctica
> aislada de nimiedades (cambio de camisa los sábados, cierta forma de
> degollar y cocinar las carnes, abstención de algunos alimentos, trato
> asiduo con los judíos en las aljamas) a los que muy a duras penas se
> podría considerar de otro modo que no sea el de meras supervivencias
> folklóricas. (Domínguez Ortiz, *Los judeoconversos en España y
> América* 151–52)

[What can be affirmed is that not all those condemned as Jews by the
Inquisition really were, since the inquisitors saw as evidence of Judaism practices, habits, and customs that not even the most sincere conversion could eradicate—such as an aversion to pork, which could not
be changed by theological arguments since it was a physiological
habit. . . . It would be serious mistake to measure this current (crypto-
Judaism) in the light of inquisitional records because greater scrutiny
of these (records) makes it increasingly doubtful that all those condemned were in any sense authentic apostates or Judaizers. The inquisitors considered as proof of apostasy trivial practices (changing a

shirt on Saturday, a certain form of slaughtering and cooking meats, abstention from some foods, assiduous contact with Jews in Jewish quarters) which could hardly be considered anything more than mere folkloric practices.]

Even acts that were only remotely related to proscribed infractions were often interpreted as evidence of Judaizing:

> Petty denunciations were the rule rather than the exception. For a neighbor to change sheets at the end of the week was sufficient proof to warrant denunciation. . . . Denunciations based on suspicion therefore led to accusations based on conjecture. (Kamen, *The Spanish Inquisition* 164)

The risk of being charged with heresy, even falsely, was great. Since the nature of a charge and the identity of the accuser were withheld, the charge was impossible to refute upon arrest. Once charged, an individual was presumed to be guilty, as Peters explains: "the very fact that the accused had been charged and arrested at all indicated that sufficient evidence for guilt had already been accumulated" (93). While awaiting trial the accused would be incarcerated, often for months or years, and was required to pay for his or her own upkeep, a situation with the potential for imposing a tremendous financial burden on family members (Kamen, *The Spanish Inquisition* 168–69). The atmosphere produced by the secretive practices of the Inquisition was undoubtedly one of suspicion and fear that any one of a number of acts might form the basis of a charge made by an unidentified individual, perhaps even a friend, neighbor, or family member (Kamen, *The Spanish Inquisition* 165).

During the 1480s tribunals were established in several Castilian cities: Sevilla and Córdoba in 1482; Toledo and Llerena in 1485; Valladolid and Murcia in 1488; and Cuenca in 1489. (In the kingdom of Aragón, tribunals were established in Zaragoza, Valencia, Barcelona, and Mallorca during the 1480s.) As the Inquisition's activities increased, so did its abuses. *Conversos* who were obviously not heretics were accused of Judaizing. The most notable case was that of Hernando de Talavera, the Archbishop of Granada and confessor to Queen Isabel, who was charged in 1506. The charge against Talavera was one of many such denunciations made by Diego Lucero, the inquisitor of Córdoba, whose discriminatory techniques had caused a great deal of alarm two years before Talavera's case, as one contemporary account explains:

> Fueron tantas las cosas deste inquisidor Lucero, que le acusaron diciendo que avía quemado muchos judíos convertidos sin aver hecho proceso conveniente contra ellos, y que a otros avía mandado tomar sus haciendas sin culpa; diciendo dél estas y otras muchas cosas. (Santa Cruz 308)

Inquisitors also launched accusations against wealthy *conversos* in order to acquire their property. The practice of confiscating an accused individual's assets was a standard procedure of the Inquisition, with the revenue going toward maintaining both those in prison and the institution itself. Although the Inquisition did not profit from this revenue, never being barely more than solvent, it subsisted on confiscations of *converso* property during much of the first century of its existence. The existence of this source of income inevitably led to corruption, and some officials were caught embezzling the proceeds (Kamen, *The Spanish Inquisition: A Historical Revision* 73–74), compounding the need for a reform of the institution.

The outcry that resulted in Talavera's acquittal in 1507 (shortly after his death) reflected a growing movement that advocated a revision of the policies and techniques of the Inquisition. Organized attempts at reforming the Inquisition emerged during the last years of Fernando's reign and continued during that of his successor, Carlos I (r. 1516–56). Although these efforts invariably met with failure, the onset of reform coincided with a reduction in the number of *conversos* who were brought before the Inquisition. Whether because the reformist movement actually began to effect a change, or because there were fewer *conversos* to persecute, available data indicate this reduction after around 1500. For example, during the first fifteen years of the institution's presence in Toledo (1485–1500), the city where the Inquisition was most active, almost twice as many trials took place than did during the next thirty years (Freund and Ruiz 181).

Perhaps the most telling statistic is the significant decline in executions remarked by Henry Kamen: "In rounded terms, it is likely that over three-quarters of all those who perished under the Inquisition in the three centuries of its existence, did so in the first twenty years" (*Inquisition and Society* 42). Of course, these decreases did not signify the end of anti-*converso* persecution in Spain. *Conversos* continued to be the principal victims of the Inquisition until the mid-1500s, and they were again targeted during the late seventeenth century (Peters 88). Purity-of-blood statutes also continued to be enacted by universities—Salamanca (1522), Valladolid (1522), and Sevilla (1537)—and by organizations such as the military order of Santiago (1555). Although only a small number of such organizations adopted statutes, their prestige was such that a Jewish lineage could mean exclusion from some of the most desirable spheres of society.

Scholars such as Peters (88) and Kamen (*Inquisition and Society* 283) argue that the first stage of the Inquisition, when it focused on *conversos*, lasted until the middle of the sixteenth century. While this may be the case, there was also a marked decline in the number of *conversos* who were brought before tribunals after the initial decades of its existence. As illustrated by the number of cases in cities such as Toledo (Kamen, *The Spanish Inquisition* 284–85) and Sevilla (Llorente 577–78), anti-*converso* persecution by the Inquisition was most severe during the 1480s and 1490s. It was when the Inquisition was in its infancy, until the onset of reform, that the alienated *converso* condition was most severely experienced. After elucidating my theoretical approach in the following chapter, I analyze the literary responses to the creation and evolution of this condition, from the heightening of tensions after the Toledo rebellion through the early years of the Inquisition, when fear of restrictive legislation and arbitrary persecution was at its peak.

2

The Theoretical Parameters
of the *Converso* Code

By the end of the fifteenth century, Spain possessed a polarized Christian society. At one end of the spectrum were the Old Christians, who believed that their superior social status (and all corresponding honors) derived from the purity of their religious lineage. At the other end were the *conversos*, whose entrance into higher social spheres was impeded by the existence of an ideological association between them and the Jews. This situation parallels more recent cases of socioreligious disenfranchisement, as the following comparison illustrates. During the fifteenth century, Fernando Álvarez de Toledo Zapata, a royal secretary to the Catholic Monarchs, was one of a number of *conversos* who attained a prominent position at court. His professional success, however, did not expunge his lineage. Although Álvarez de Toledo Zapata's son, Antonio, became a page to Prince Juan, Antonio was marginalized within the prince's retinue because he was not considered a pure Christian, as the following passage from Gonzalo Fernández de Oviedo y Valdés's *Libro de la cámara real* implies:

> En el tiempo del Príncipe, mi señor, en su mesa e despensa e cozina e copa e botillería, ni en otro offiçio alguno, que se exerçitase de la puerta adentro de palaçio, no cupo hombre que no fuesse castizo hijo dalgo, limpio o a lo menos christiano viejo, si no fueron dos o tres, que no quiero dezir, e que los avía resçibido la Reyna antes quel Príncipe tuviesse su casa e libros aparte; *e aquesos eran muy conosçidos como por extraños del rebaño de su graçia.* (Alcalá and Sanz 111, emphasis added)

In modern times, Christians with a Jewish lineage have had a similar type of Otherness imposed on them. A noteworthy case is that of Madeleine Albright, who, during the 1990s, served first as the U.S. ambassador to the United Nations and then as Secretary of State under President Clinton. Although she was raised a Catholic during World War II and in Communist Europe (before fleeing with her family to the United States), Albright's Jewish heritage was revealed shortly after she was nominated for the position of secretary of state. (Her paternal grandparents are thought to have perished at Auschwitz.) This revelation immediately caused the news media to speculate that she might be biased when dealing with the Middle East. The analogy between Albright and the *conversos* derives from the manner by which both were stigmatized by association with the Other. In other words, Albright's motivations in dealing with the Middle East were scrutinized because she was associated with Judaism (specifically, with American Jews' support for Israel), not because she was a practicing Jew herself (as she was not). Like the *conversos* of the fifteenth century, Albright had Jewishness imposed upon her because of her lineage.

Of course, the discrimination faced by late-medieval converts from Judaism to Christianity and their descendants was different in some ways from that experienced during the twentieth century. For example, *conversos* did not face discrimination based on skin color. At the same time, regardless of the criteria by which individuals are defined collectively as the Other, medieval and modern manifestations of discrimination involve impositions of Otherness based on indelible stigmas that prevent seamless assimilation. To cite another contemporary example, in spite of his accomplishments on the field, Jackie Robinson is most remembered as the first African American to play Major League baseball, a label that essentially imposes on him the same racial stigma that once excluded African Americans from playing at that level.

The imposition of Otherness often resonates in the literature of those who have been marginalized. Examples of such literature have been evaluated by Homi Bhabha, who identifies an "unhomeliness"—that is, an awareness by the marginalized individual of being socially displaced—"in fictions that negotiate the powers of cultural difference in a range of transhistorical sites" (Bhabha 9). Bhabha examines the presence of unhomeliness in Toni Morrison's novel *Beloved*, a work that exposes the persecution of blacks by emphasizing the "historical and discursive boundaries of slavery" (16). In the following chapters, I also define a manner by which literary texts underscore the boundaries of a marginal condition imposed by an oppressive majority. In the texts I consider, the expression of these boundaries is seen in metaphors that recall the nature and trajectory of anti-

converso discrimination, a corpus of metaphors that I collectively term the *converso* code.

In the formulation of my theoretical model, I endeavor to apply the principles and terminology of semiotics to the analysis of literary texts. Although semiotics is not an innovative method of literary interpretation, it does provide an innovative and appropriate perspective for examining the particular texts informed by the *converso* code. The *converso* code is found in literary language that, like any language, communicates meaning through associations of interdependent linguistic elements. This is a fundamental communicative feature of language, as Jonathan Culler explains: "What makes each element of a language what it is, what gives it its identity, are the contrasts between it and other elements within the system of the language" (57). Semiotics is concerned with identifying the meaning assigned to contrasts between linguistic elements, these elements being components of what has traditionally been called a sign.

A sign, as Roland Barthes explains, is formed by

> a relation between two terms, a signifier and a signified. . . . We must here be on our guard for despite common parlance which simply says that the signifier *expresses* the signified, we are dealing, in any semiological system, not with two, but with three different terms. For what we grasp is not all one term after the other, but the correlation which unites them: there are, therefore, the signifier, the signified and the sign, which is the associative total of the first two terms. Take a bunch of roses: I use it to *signify* my passion. Do we have here, then, only a signifier and a signified, the roses and my passion? Not even that: to put it accurately, there are here only "passionified" roses. (112–13)

In Barthes's example, this "associative total" (or sign) refers to the meaning assigned to the correlation between a term and an abstract concept: Barthes's "roses" form part of a sign when they are ideologically linked to the notion of "passion." Two additional examples are found in a statement, "God will provide a way" (9), examined by Floyd Merrell, a more recent scholar in the field. In this statement, the terms "God" and "way" form parts of associative totals, that is, signs that communicate connections between terms and their "symbolic implication[s]" (Merrell 19). "God" and "way" function as signifiers when the interpreter of the statement associates "God" with the concept of an omnipotent force and "way" with the inspiration that is said to come to the individual who believes that faith in

Providence can surmount obstacles. As such, "God" is a signifier whose link to a signified (the abstract notion of an omnipotent force) creates a sign that symbolizes a traditional conception of God. Likewise, "way" is a signifier that corresponds to a signified (the abstract notion of divine inspiration) in order to yield an associative total that symbolizes the concept of faith.

Other types of associations involve terms that are best considered as components of a "semion" (Merrell 19), that is, a sign that involves an association that undergoes "metaphorical concretion" in being "available to empirical observation" (Merrell 21). Although he does not differentiate between the notions of sign and semion, Barthes provides what may be considered as an example of the latter in his discussion of the statement "because my name is lion" (115–16): "Inasmuch as it is addressed to me, a pupil in the second form, it tells me clearly: I am a grammatical example meant to illustrate the rule about the agreement of the predicate. . . . [The statement's] true and fundamental signification is to impose itself on me as the presence of a certain agreement of the predicate. I conclude that I am faced with a particular, greater, semiological system, since it is co-extensive with the language: there is, indeed, a signifier . . . (*my name is lion*). . . . there is a signified (*I am a grammatical example*) and there is a global signification, which is none other than the correlation of the signifier and the signified; for neither the naming of the lion nor the grammatical example are given separately" (116). Here "my name is lion" becomes a signifier when it is concretized, that is, when it is considered in a particular (scholastic) context in relation to its signifier, "I am a grammatical example."

In Barthes's example, "my name is lion" and "I am a grammatical example" do not form an associative total (a phrase that I borrow from Barthes and use as a synonym for semion) unless their relationship is contextualized. In the absence of such concretization, the terms that participate in Barthes's association have no relation to each other semantically. Semionic concretization may also derive from syntactic links between normally unrelated terms. As Merrell explains, "God will provide a way" and "the shepherd leading his sheep to water," which are dissimilar in a semantic sense, become parts of a semion when they are included in a statement such as "God will provide a way 'like' the shepherd leading his sheep to water" (21). In this statement, the associative total of the correlation between the signifier "God will provide a way" and the signified "the shepherd leading his sheep to water" is a less abstract or concretized notion of God. In another statement discussed by Merrell, "The universe is (like) a machine" (19), the link between the signifier "universe" and the signified "machine," terms that allude to completely different things in everyday speech, inspires a metaphor for the mechanical manner by which the universe is commonly said to operate. The utterer of the statement "The universe is (like) a machine" considers an abstract notion (the universe) in a nonabstract (mechanical) sense, and this concretization enlists the association between the two terms as a semion.

Semions may involve elements that are not only semantically dissimilar; they may possess opposite meanings. Those I study consist of antithetical signifiers and signifieds, the employment of such contradictory discourse being an essential component of poetry, as Yury Lotman explains: "The poetic world has thus not only its own vocabulary, but its own system of synonyms and antonyms. Thus, in some texts 'love' can be a synonym of 'life,' whereas in others it is a synonym of 'death.' In a poetic text, 'day' and 'night,' or 'life' and 'death' can be synonyms" (85). Antithetical associations gain meaning in poetry, according to Lotman (114, 119, 123), when they are repeated at both the intratextual and intertextual levels. By extension, the meaning of these repeated associations is said to be valid when they are seen as pertaining to a system, which is defined by the consistent revelation of this meaning (in one or more texts) according to a uniformly applied set of criteria. In semionic terms, associative totals of correlations of semantically unrelated lexical entities become valid metaphors when they form part of such a system (Merrell 19).

Barthes asserts that "all criticism must consent to the *ascesis*, to the artifice of analysis; and in analysis, it must match method and language" (112). My method consists of focusing on the placement in texts of lexical entities that suggest an associative total, or semion, that metaphorically alludes to different images of alienated *conversos*. In the chapters that follow, I identify the antithetical terms that produce these semions and explain the manner by which the metaphors recall characteristic features of the inferior social and religious conditions of the *conversos*. Furthermore, as I demonstrate through consistent evaluation of these semions according to the same basic criteria, the *converso* code, the phrase by which I collectively refer to the semions, is actually a series of interrelated systems that parallel the historical trajectory of the disenfranchisement of the *conversos*.

Each of these semions is composed of a direct or implied reference to a particular *converso* or to the *conversos* in general (signifier), which is linked to a reference to a Jew, a Jewish object, or a distinctive feature of the Jewishness by which *conversos* were identified as inferior (signified). The semion created by this correlation, involving terms that are semantically dissimilar (inasmuch as a Jew is not a Christian), is a metaphorical representation of a "Jewish" Christian. The purity-of-blood statutes restricted *conversos* from entering public spheres because of their Jewish heritage, and the activities of the Inquisition intensified suspicion of them because, like Jews, they were perceived as foreign to the Catholic identity that Spain was in the process of forging for itself. Although neither the statutes nor the Inquisition directly affected most *conversos*, any *converso* was a potential victim of discrimination and persecution because the possession of a Jewish ancestry circumscribed an individual as an inferior Christian. Whether they are explicit or oblique, the semions in the *converso* code speak to the potential for such oppression to occur through allusions to images of alienated *conversos*.

My use of the term "code" is not meant to imply that the writers I study created a secret discourse that was only comprehensible to *conversos*. The meaning of the semions in the *converso* code might have been discerned by both Old and New Christian readers, especially those who were familiar with *cancionero* poetry. Indeed, the *converso* code is formed by semions that resemble the conceits (*conceptos*) often found in fifteenth-century courtly verse (as well as in contemporary prose). Like the semions I examine, these conceits can involve antithetical terms that achieve a metaphorical significance through their association.[1] Conceits frequently appear in love poems, such as the "Esparsa suya en que descubre las propiedades del amor," a work by a *converso*, Rodrigo Cota, with whom I deal at length in Chapters 4 and 6.[2] In this poem, Cota places in opposition several phrases composed of antithetical terms in order to inspire a typical *cancionero* allusion to the "carácter contradictorio de la pasión" (contradictory nature of passion) (Alonso 23):

> Vista ciega, luz escura,
> gloria triste, vida muerta,
> ventura de desuentura,
> lloro alegre, risa incierta,
> hiel sabrosa, dulce agrura,
> paz y yra y saña presta
> es amor, con vestidura
> de gloria que pena cuesta. (*Cancionero castellano* 588)

The major difference between this type of discourse and the semions in the *converso* code is the nature of the allusions that are produced: rather than evoking abstract notions, the semions in the *converso* code are socially concretized. Even when they were presented more obliquely, as in the *converso* laments I study in Chapters 6 and 7, these semions would have been potentially understood by any reader with a knowledge of the social tensions between Old and New Christians and the nature of contemporary literary devices.

At the same time, there are instances when readers would have needed knowledge of an individual *converso*'s circumstances in order to comprehend certain social themes. In particular, this information would have been possessed by those who engaged in poetic dialogues with Juan Poeta (Chapter 3) and those able to decipher the micro-allegory in Rodrigo Cota's "Diálogo entre el Amor y un Viejo" (Chapter 6). During the course of this book pertinent information about individual *conversos* is taken into account to the extent that it complements and enhances my readings of the texts.

Some scholars might argue that in suggesting the existence of a *converso* code, I am myself guilty of participating in the creation of the marginalized *converso*. According to Paul Julian Smith, "even critics who are sympathetic to Jews and *conversos* find it hard to abandon (or even to recognize) habits of mind they share with the anti-Semites: an essentialist conception of the Jew or *converso*, determined by a faith in the 'objectivity' of an unacknowledged hierarchy, itself legitimized by a universal 'human nature' which is in fact constructed according to dominant (non-Jewish) criteria" (29). Smith points out one of the major problems of past studies dealing with *converso* literature, namely, the tendency to see *converso* works as ideologically linked to their author's supposed religious tendencies. Such a notion is evident in Castro's assertion that works by *conversos* ranging from Alonso de Cartagena to Santa Teresa "debe[n] al pueblo judío" ([are] indebted to the Jewish people) (*La realidad* 50). More recently, the same concept informs Nepaulsingh's readings of *Lazarillo de Tormes, El Abencerraje,* and *Los siete libros de la Diana* and Faur's treatment of *converso* writers as "Jews [who] had no idea of the norms and ideologies regulating life in the Christian world" (2). Unlike these views, my conception of the *converso* code does not assume that literature will reveal an author's relationship to his Jewish past. In other words, the *converso* code is not composed of semions that reveal the existence of individual crypto-Jews or sincere Christians. It is composed of semions that metaphorically allude to how any *converso* could be treated as a second-class Christian regardless of his or her religious sincerity.

The ensuing chapters trace the evolution of these semions parallel to the progressive intensification in anti-*converso* hostility during the fifteenth century, from the years following the Toledo rebellion through the 1490s. While the changing sociopolitical climate contributed to divergences among the terms and phrases used in works that express the *converso* code, the homogeneity of this corpus of literary voices is found in its depictions of the Jewishness imposed on *conversos*. It should again be underscored that such depictions may not be interpreted as reflections of actual religious beliefs. Specifically, although certain expressions of the *converso* code by two writers to be considered, Antón de Montoro and Rodrigo Cota (and to a lesser extent those of Juan Poeta), suggest that they attempted to embrace Christianity, such literary discourse does not, by itself, serve as a spiritual barometer. By focusing on the boundaries that defined the inferior status of New Christians, the *converso* code does allude to the way *conversos* were treated within a predominantly Old Christian society. As such, the *converso* code is an "articulation of difference" (2), to use Bhabha's phrase, that evokes, from different perspectives and at different historical moments, images of disenfranchised *conversos*.

The Poetic Dialogues Involving Juan Poeta

The corpus of works involving Juan de Valladolid presents the greatest variety of contexts in which the *converso* code is manifested. Valladolid, known in literature as Juan Poeta, was probably born during the first decade of the fifteenth century (Rubio González 101), of humble origins. Antón de Montoro (c. 1404–c. 1477), a contemporary *converso* poet who was also of the working class (a tailor),[1] sheds light on Poeta's family background in "Montoro al dicho Juan Poeta, porque pedió dineros al cabildo":

> Pues ¿sabéys quién es su padre?:
> un verdugo, pregonero,
> y ¿queréys reýr?, su madre
> criada de un mesonero[.] (Ciceri 184)

Evidence found in several poems that I examine further on in this chapter suggests that Poeta was born into the Jewish faith. In "Coplas del conde de Paredes a Juan Poeta cuando le cautivaron moros en Fez," Pedro Manrique alleges that, after being captured by Muslim pirates, Poeta requested to be circumcised in order to ingratiate himself with his Muslim captors. However, the operation was unnecessary because the request was actually made in order to demonstrate to the Muslims that, like them, he had already been circumcised:

> Pedistes circuncisión.
> Todo el pueblo fue venido
> y con muy gran alarido
> truxeron carbón molido,
> tijeras y navajón,
> y vos, puesto en gran estrecho,
> dexistes con gran plazer:
> "Sabé todos que está hecho

esto que queréis hacer."

. . . .

    Diz que dixo el alfaquí[2]
"Escusado es mi trabajo,
pues de revés ni de tajo
no hallo en este retajo
qué pueda cortar de aquí.
Si lo hizo algún rabí,
Dios le dé buena ventura,
y si lo hizo natura,
mayor hecho nunca vi." (*Cancionero de obras* 88)

In "Coplas del conde de Paredes a Juan Poeta, en una perdonança en Valencia," Rodrigo Manrique makes a similar allusion when he claims that Poeta was circumcised "otra vez":

El cáliz del consagrar
se quiso hazer cuchillo
para vos circuncidar
otra vez, y recortar
un poco más del capillo. (Rodríguez Puértolas, *Poesía crítica* 291)

In an anonymous work, "Otra a Juan Poeta hecha por un cauallero que estando jugando le demandó que le diesse algo y él le dio una dobla quebrada y una copla que dezía," the author makes the same inference by comparing the procedure ("lo que a vos hizo el rabí") to the pairing of a coin ("dobla quebrada") by a silversmith ("platero"):

    Por hauerme importunado
os do essa dobla quebrada
ques razón que al retajado
que gela den retajada
y nos espantéys grossero
poeta juan tarabí
pues que le hizo el platero
lo que a vos hizo el rabí. (*Segunda parte* 188)

If these allegations are accurate, Poeta may have adopted Christianity during his early childhood, perhaps during the wave of conversions between 1412 and 1416.

    In spite of his modest beginnings, Poeta was able to find a place within the highest social circles. After possibly serving as a customs official in

Palermo between 1422 and 1444, he entered the service of King Juan II in the early 1450s, and he was at Queen Isabel's court in 1477.[3] Information regarding the last years of his life is sparse. Roth places him in Toledo and Córdoba during the early 1480s (172), and he likely died soon afterward.

Poeta was an active participant in the poetic rivalries that occurred within courtly circles throughout the 1400s. In general, during the first half of the century these rivalries, which often involved assaults on an opponent's habits or literary talent, "no son invectivas sino vehículos para destacar la listeza del poeta" (are not invectives but vehicles designed to show off the cleverness of the poet) (Scholberg 257). Even when such exchanges became socioreligious in nature, with a *converso* or Old Christian poet pointing out the Jewish lineage of a rival, they are usually continuations of a longstanding medieval tradition whereby "trovadores o juglares quisieron demostrar su talento para el insulto" (troubadours or minstrels wanted to demonstrate their ability to insult) (Scholberg 339).[4] Poeta, and to a lesser extent Montoro, became central figures in these exchanges during the latter part of the century in the poems they wrote and in others directed to them by Old Christians. It is my opinion that the recurrent focus of these exchanges on the *converso* lineages of these two poets represents an awareness of the disenfranchisement of the *conversos* after 1449.

The image of the alienated *converso* is produced in an interchange between Poeta and Montoro that most likely occurred during the early 1450s. The assignation of this date derives from allusions made both in the work by Montoro that inspired the exchange and in Poeta's response. In the former, "A Juan de Valladolid, aconsejándole," Montoro situates Poeta "En esa corte real / donde vos pensáis valer" (Ciceri 177). Although Montoro could be alluding to Poeta's tenure at the court of Queen Isabel, it is more probable that the "corte real" is either that of King Juan II or Enrique IV during the mid-1450s. In 1455 Poeta was in Córdoba as part of the retinue of the Marqués de Villena, where he may have attended the wedding of King Enrique IV (Rubio González 104) and where he may also have come into contact with Montoro, who resided in that city. It is reasonable to speculate that Poeta, who made a career out of service to the monarchy and the nobility, attempted to gain favor at the court of the recently crowned king, to which Montoro's poem would refer. The exchange most likely took place in the wake of the uprisings in Toledo and Ciudad Real and the promulgation of the first purity-of-blood statutes, that is, after the *conversos* had become the objects of violent persecution and legal discrimination based on a perception that they were inferior Christians.

In "A Juan de Valladolid" Montoro establishes a link between himself and Poeta with a semion that identifies them as Christians who carry the stigma of possessing a Jewish ancestry:

> Juan, señor y grande amigo,
> con mi coraçón muy sano
> vos quiero dar un castigo,
>
> . . . .
>
> por ser vos y yo judíos
> vuestros enojos son míos
> y mis daños también vuestros. (Ciceri 176)

Because Poeta and Montoro (signifiers as the subjects of "vos y yo," respectively) are considered to be "judíos" (signified) they share the same "enojos" and "daños," terms that might reflect a resentment ("enojos") caused by the injurious treatment ("daños") they have endured. As in each of the semions considered in this chapter, the association between the signifiers and the signified, in this case between two Christian individuals and the term "judíos," defines the inferior *converso* condition.

Poeta adopts an offensive posture in his response to Montoro, "Respuesta de Juan de Valladolid," by employing a semion that scornfully associates Montoro with his Jewish lineage: "Malicioso desigual, / más malo que Lucifer, / judío del general" (Ciceri 179). In these lines, a signifier that references the inferiority of a Christian individual (Montoro), "Malicioso desigual," is linked to a signified, "judío," that defines this inferiority in a genealogical sense. The link between these terms evokes the same notion of a Jewish Christian that is depicted in Montoro's poem.

In another work, "Coplas que enbió Juan Poeta a Gómez Manrrique desde Aragón," most likely composed between 1455 and 1458, when he was in that region (Rubio González 104), Poeta recounts his participation in a pig hunt. During the hunt he wounds a sow ("puerca") and captures her seven piglets ("siete lechones") (*Cancionero castellano* 106). Like a mendicant who hoards any scrap of food he encounters, Poeta hides the pigs in a synagogue ("sinoga") rather than eat the meat immediately:

> Y como faze el mendigo
> quando tiene alguna boga,
> que non da della a su amigo,
> con vn celemín de trigo
> los encerré enla sinoga[.] (*Cancionero castellano* 106)

The image of the pigs confined in a synagogue constitutes a direct insult on the Jews by mocking the biblical law that prohibits them from eating pork. This image is one of two that dissociates Poeta from his Jewish past. The second takes shape in the following lines, in which a Jew inquires how Poeta has managed to make such a sacrifice, that is, how he could completely forsake the faith of his ancestors by participating in the hunt and hiding the pigs in a synagogue:

> y el linaje de Macán[5]
> vino a mí con gran bollicio
> con dolor y con afán:
> "¿Cómo vos, poeta Juan,
> fezistes tal sacreficio?" (*Cancionero castellano* 106)

Poeta responds by ridiculing the Jews once again, this time by evoking the Old Testament episode (Exod. 32) in which the Jews worshiped a golden calf, which he mistakenly labels a "bezerro de plata":

> Respondíles por su daño
> el caso que se relata:
> "Vos otros con gran engaño
> adorastes dios estraño
> con el bezerro de plata;
> y pues soys tan desonestos
> contra mí que bien me rijo,
> judíos, groseros cestos,
> fazed sacrificio destos
> como Abrahan de su hijo.["] (*Cancionero castellano* 106)

The implication in these derisive lines is that, because they are heretics themselves, the Jews should not be offended because their synagogue has been desecrated. The involvement of an incident that represents the greatest sin committed by the biblical Jews may be an attempt by Poeta to assert the superiority of his own identity as a practicing Christian (who willingly consumes food that is prohibited by Jewish law). However, one might just as well speculate that Poeta's motivation in composing this satirical poem was less than pious inasmuch as his satirical tone is typical of contemporary poetic exchanges (Scholberg 263–64).

Of course, it is impossible to determine whether Poeta is merely mocking the Jews in "Coplas que enbió . . . a Gómez Manrrique" or employing a satirical tone in order to insist, somewhat desperately, that he is a sincere

Christian. In either case, the poem forms part of a dialogue that exemplifies the futility for a *converso* of dissociating himself from his Jewish past. In the reply, "Respuesta de Gómez Manrrique a Juan Poeta," Gómez Manrique, an Old Christian, demonstrates this futility by underscoring Poeta's intrinsic Otherness. Manrique calls Poeta "no judío ni cristiano, / mas excelente marrano" (*Cancionero castellano* 107), verses that function as a semionic metaphor for Poeta's marginal status as a Christian. Since the late fourteenth century the term "marrano" had been used as a synonym for *converso* in order to express a general mistrust, among Old Christians and Jews, of the religious sincerity of Jews who had converted (Roth 3). By involving Poeta in this stereotype, Manrique's semion, the associative total of the correlation between "marrano" and the phrase "no judío ni cristiano," perpetuates the image of the disenfranchised *converso* in contemporary terms. In this sense, "marrano," a signifier that alludes to Poeta, is defined as "no judío ni cristiano," a signified that reflects a late fifteenth-century manner of depicting inferiority based on lineage. As Roth observes (229), similar terms were used by the royal chronicler Andrés Bernáldez to describe "la mayor parte" of the *converso* population, who, in Bernáldez's opinion, "no eran ni judíos ni christianos" (599).

Gómez's brother, Rodrigo, the first Count of Paredes, reviles Poeta in a previously discussed poem, "Coplas del conde de Paredes a Juan Poeta, en una perdonança en Valencia," most likely written a little more than a decade later. Rodrigo explicitly evokes the lineage of Poeta in a deprecatory tone through a series of semions consisting of correlations between terms and phrases that reference Poeta as a Christian who is tainted by his Jewish lineage. In the work Poeta attends a "perdonança" in a church in Valencia,[6] probably the one that took place in 1470 (Rodríguez Puértolas, *Poesía crítica* 289), when Poeta is thought to have visited that city (Rubio González 104). Because Poeta enters the church ("en vos venir," "sólo por la vuestra entrada"), Christian objects change into Jewish ones:

> Juan Poeta, en vos venir
> en estas santas pisadas,
> muchas cosas consagradas
> d'un ser en otro tornadas
> las heziste convertir.
> La bula del Padre Santo,
> dada por nuestra salud,
> metida so vuestro manto
> se tornó con gran quebranto

escritura del Talmud.

Y la muy devota iglesia
sólo por la vuestra entrada
fue luego contaminada,
en ese punto tornada
casa santa de ley vieja,
y el cuerpo del Redentor,
que llagastes vos con hierro,
del vuestro puro temor,
sudando sangre y sudor
se tornó luego bezerro.

El bulto de la Señora,
la Virgen nuestra abogada,
por mejor ser adorada
y de vos más acatada,
hízose una rica Tora.
El cáliz del consagrar
se quiso hazer cuchillo
para vos circuncidar
otra vez, y recortar
un poco más del capillo.

No dexemos la patena
a que la boca llegastes,
que luego que la besastes
se dize que la tornastes
caçuela con berenjena.
El ara, qu'es consagrada
y de piedra dura, fina,
de vuestra mano tocada
en un punto fue tornada
ataifor con adafina. (Rodríguez Puértolas, *Poesía crítica* 290–91)

The semions are formed by correspondences between signifiers that name Christian objects and signifieds that denote those into which they are transformed: "bula del Padre Santo"[7] / "escritura del Talmud,"[8] "hierro / bezerro,"[9] "bulto de la Señora / Tora,"[10] "cáliz / cuchillo para vos circuncidar," "patena / caçuela con berenjena,"[11] "ara / ataifor con adafina."[12] By extension, these correspondences metaphorically allude to the inferior condition of the *converso* who is responsible for the transformations. In other words, the changes are provoked by Poeta's mere presence in the church, that is, because he cannot escape the lineage that devalues his Christianity. Further on in this poem Rodrigo accuses Poeta of having recited Jewish prayers on Saturday (that is, on the Jewish Sabbath), behaving as if he were a rabbi:

> El sábado no vos vi,
> qu'estovistes encerrado,
> en oración ocupado,
> presumiendo de letrado,
> enfingiendo de rabí. (Rodríguez Puértolas, *Poesía crítica* 294)

Once again Poeta, the subject of the signifier "vos," is treated as a Jew in being associated with the signified "rabí," an association that is enhanced by the mention that he was praying on Saturday, the Jewish Sabbath.

While at various Italian courts in the 1470s Poeta came into contact with Suero de Ribera, who composed a poem to commemorate their encounter ("Coplas de Ribera a Juan Poeta, estando los dos en Nápoles"). In this work, Poeta's father first creates the association between Poeta and his Jewish lineage while speaking with Ribera:

> yo hallé en la costanilla
> vuestro padre pregonando,
> y dezía en sus pregones
> . . . .
>   Toquéle luego la mano,
> díxele de vos gran bien.
> Él me dixo: "Dezí, hermano,
> ¿es mi hijo allá cristiano
> o de la ley de Mosén?
> Y teniendo en esta empresa
> han quemado un nieto mío,
> que por su causa me pesa,
> que tienen su mujer presa
> y dizen que es él judío." (*Cancionero de obras* 120)

Poeta's Jewish lineage is evoked here through a semion in which "hijo," a signifier that designates Poeta, is associated with the signified "cristiano o de la ley de Mosén." The associative total of the correlation between "hijo" and "cristiano o de la ley de Mosén," a signified composed of terms similar to those used by Gómez Manrique (in "Respuesta . . . a Juan Poeta") and Bernáldez, is a metaphor for Poeta's *converso* identity.

The declaration in the lines above by Poeta's father, "y dizen que es él judío," appears to contain a signified, "judío," that reflects another common manner of defining the religious character of *conversos* (by equating them with Jews). As such, the term, through its correlation to the signifier "él" (which refers to Poeta's nephew in the poem, who was presumably also a *converso*), participates in a semion that underscores the *converso* identity of Poeta's nephew. Furthermore, the description of the punishments meted out to Poeta's nephew and his wife ("su mujer") may indicate the year the poem was composed. If the term "quemado" alludes to the inquisitional punishment of burning at the stake, then this poem could not have been written until after the first auto-de-fé was carried out in Sevilla in 1481. This possibility is enhanced by the reference to the imprisonment ("presa") of "su mujer," which also infers that the work dates from after tribunals began to drag family members into their nets. As allusions to punishments meted out by the Inquisition, the terms "quemado" and "presa" are signifieds whose respective associations to the signifiers "nieto" and "mujer" undergo "metaphorical concretion[s]" (Merrell 21) through their links to a particular context, that is, anti-*converso* persecution after 1480.

It is not surprising that Ribera involves Poeta's father in his discriminatory discourse. In the previously discussed "Coplas que enbió Juan Poeta a Gómez Manrrique desde Aragón" Poeta himself insinuates that his father may have been a practicing Jew (after conversion?). While Poeta eagerly participates in the pig hunt, his father always refrained from such activities, the inference being that Poeta is more Christian than his father: "que mi padre e mi señor / jamás no fue caçador, / mas es lo su fijo agora" (*Cancionero castellano* 106).

Further on in "Coplas de Ribera" the author describes an encounter between Poeta and Montoro:

> Y también mucho furioso
> que dize como de un moro,
> esse hombre muy famoso,
> poeta muy copioso,
> llamado Antón de Montoro
> que vos con cara que toca,
> odre hinchado con pajuelas,
> según la nariz os toca[.] (*Cancionero de obras* 121)

As Jauralde Pou observes, "Era creencia común que la nariz de los judíos se distinguía por sus exageradas dimensiones o desproporción" [it was a common belief that Jewish noses were distinguished by their exaggerated dimensions or disproportion] (*Cancionero de obras* 121, note 12). In the lines above, this anti-Jewish stigma, expressed as "según la nariz os toca" (meaning the way Montoro's nose touches Poeta), contains a signified, "nariz" (referring to a stereotypically "Jewish" nose), whose link to its Christian signifier, "Antón de Montoro," projects a stigma of religious inferiority on Montoro.

The aforementioned poem written after Poeta's capture by Muslim pirates, "Coplas del conde de Paredes a Juan Poeta cuando le cautivaron moros en Fez," was not written before 1476 given that the probable author, Pedro Manrique, did not become the second count of Paredes until that year (Cortina, *Jorge Manrique,* 132). According to Pedro, when he was captured Poeta was on a pilgrimage to the Holy Land, ostensibly in order to establish contact with the Jews:

> Si de moros fuestes pre(s)a,
> ordenólo Dios muy bien.
> Vuestro ardid era Judea;
> la fama, Jerusalém. (*Cancionero de obras* 87)

This alleged pilgrimage to a geographic region that is traditionally identified with the Jewish people foreshadows other semions that evoke Poeta's inferior *converso* condition. In the lines that follow, Pedro describes the consequences of Poeta's failed pilgrimage in terms lifted from the Old Testament:

> Sacaros de la prisión
> a do estávades en Fez
> a Dios fue cosa raéz,[13]
> como hizo la otra vez,
> de poder de faraón. (*Cancionero de obras* 87)

The association of Poeta's captivity with that of the Jews in Egypt (Exod. 1–12), suggested by the reference to the Egyptian ruler ("faraón"), creates a link between Poeta and the biblical Jews.[14] The term "prisión" is, therefore, a signifier that recalls Poeta (in the sense that it refers to Poeta's captivity) in connection with the captivity of the Jews in Egypt (Exod. 1–12), which is referenced by the signified "poder de faraón." This correlation is enhanced by the allegation that Poeta was taken prisoner while on a journey to the Holy Land, which was, of course, the ultimate destination of the Jews after they were released from bondage. Moreover, Poeta's journey is thwarted by an obstacle: "Cuando vistes que la mar / por carreras no se abría"

(*Cancionero de obras* 87). In recalling the Red Sea, which temporarily impeded the departure of the biblical Jews (Exod. 14), these lines also embellish the allusion to Poeta's socioreligious inferiority.

Further on in the poem Pedro volunteers to assist Poeta in completing his journey. Pedro is eager to "daros passo en el Jordán" (*Cancionero de obras* 89), that is, the Jordan River. According to Pedro, this is a fitting route for Poeta to follow inasmuch as it is the same one taken by "los hijos de Abraham" (*Cancionero de obras* 90) as they also made their way to the Holy Land after their wanderings in the desert (Joshua 1). Once again, an Old Testament reference ("hijos de Abraham") is a signified that, in being linked to Poeta (to whom the corresponding signifier "os" in "daros passo" refers), participates in a metaphor that alludes to his heritage. Poeta, a Christian, is identified with Jews ("hijos de Abraham"), a perpetuation of the contemporary perception of *conversos* as second-class Christians.

Forced to remain in Fez, Poeta decides to adopt the ways of the Muslims in order to appease his captors:

> diz que dixistes un día,
> como varón que tenía
> nuestra fe en el carcañal
> con esperanza muy seca:
> "¡Biva, biva Mahoma!
> Más vale casa de Meca
> que no la corte de Roma." (*Cancionero de obras* 88)

Poeta's alleged religious inconstancy is reinforced by the declaration that he has three wives, whose names (and the symbols with which they are associated: the cross, the Torah, and the Koran, and the three masculine names several lines later) represent Poeta's vacillation among Christianity, Judaism, and Islam:

> no por grandes menesteres
> marido de tres mujeres:
> Marina, Jamila y Axa.
> Aunque está agora en calma,
> sobre vos debatirán
> —y, a la fin, sobre vuestra alma—
> cruz y tora y alcorán.
> De cómo vos llamarán
> dexarés fama y renombre,
> no seyendo más de un hombre

cada cual de ellas su nombre:
Juan, Simuel y Reduán. (*Cancionero de obras* 93)

Poeta's alliance with two of these faiths, Islam and Christianity, is motivated in the poem by self-interest. He adopts Islam in order to save his life
and Christianity because of the advantages it affords in contemporary
Spanish society. However, according to Pedro, Poeta is a Jew at heart:

Moro, por no ser muerto;
cristiano, por más valer;
pero judío es lo cierto,
a lo que puedo saber. (*Cancionero de obras* 93)

In these lines, Poeta, the subject of the signifier "vos" (in the above-men-
tioned verse "De cómo vos llamarán"), is linked to Judaism by the correlation between "vos" and its signified, "judío," the manner by which others
will most assuredly ("lo cierto") denominate him ("vos llamarán"). This
semion is reinforced by another in the final stanza that again labels Poeta
inferior by linking him (inasmuch as he is the implied subject and therefore the signifier) to a signified, "Yahudí,"[15] that denotes a Jew: "Yahudí
desventurado" (*Cancionero de obras* 94).

Poeta's capture by Muslim pirates must have been an event of some
notoriety. It also inspired a poem by Pedro's uncle, Gómez Manrique
("Otras trobas de Gómez Manrrique a Juan Poeta quando le catiuaron los
moros dallende") that was probably composed around the same time as
"Coplas del conde de Paredes." The work includes several semions that
identify Poeta as a "Jewish" Christian. One of these characterizes him as
such by comparing Poeta's condition as a neophyte to Gómez's own religious purity: "Poeta, vos soys nouicio, / que quiere dezir confeso / yo soy
antiguo profeso" (*Cancionero castellano* 100). In the semion created in
these verses, the Christian identity of Poeta, the subject of the signifier
"vos," is defined as different (read inferior) because he is a "nouicio" and a
"confeso," two signifieds that stand in opposition to Gomez's declaration
that he is personally an "antiguo profeso" (Old Christian). Another semion, in a verse that reads "el mayor delos ebreos" (*Cancionero castellano*
100), openly links Poeta, the subject of the signifier "mayor," to his Jewish
lineage, recalled by the signified "delos ebreos," which once again denotes
the common perception of *conversos* as Jewish Christians. A third semion
used to underscore Poeta's *converso* condition in this poem is slightly
more oblique. It occurs in Gómez's accusation that Poeta is a "Trobador syn
capirote" (*Cancionero castellano* 100). The term "capirote" (meaning

conical hood) may be interpreted as an allusion to the prepuce. Poeta (to whom the signifier "Trobador" refers) is "syn capirote," this phrase being a signified that, in alluding to the Jewish act of circumcision and being linked to Poeta, once again serves as a metaphor for his socioreligious condition.

Although the final four poems I consider in this chapter are more difficult to situate chronologically, they also appear to have been composed during the second half of the fifteenth century. This is the case with Gómez Manrique's "Coplas de Gómez Manrrique a Johan Poeta, que le demandaua pan en su tierra, e dezía que le auía librado el arçobispo quatrocientas fanegas de trigo enel arçiprestazgo de Halía," which was most likely written late in Poeta's life. This chronological placement of the poem is suggested by Manrique's description of Poeta's wealth, which he probably would have not possessed until he was an adult since he was born into a working-class family:

> Que más da su señoría
>   en vn día
> que suman todas mis rentas;
> digo por las quatroçientas
>   o quinientas
> que tenéys en Halía[.] (*Cancionero castellano* 130)

Further on, Manrique underscores Poeta's lineage without mentioning it explicitly, during the course of an attack on Poeta's literary talent:

> Mas sy yo no deuaneo,
>   cierto creo
> que esta vuestra poesýa
> saltará en mercaduría
>   todavía
> según las señales veo.
> Destas señales nonbradas
> no declaro su blasón,
> por quanto por la razón
> sacaréys ser coloradas. (*Cancionero castellano* 130)

As Scholberg indicates, these verses conceal a reference to Poeta's heritage: "Aluden a su judaísmo al decirle que [sus obras] son coloradas como las señales que llevaban los judíos" (Allude to his Jewishness by telling him that [his works] are colored like the emblems worn by Jews) (340–41).

A similar reference that alludes to Spanish Jews living in Italy is found in *Retrato de la Lozana andaluza* (1528), when Beatriz identifies them as "Aquellos que llevan aquella señal colorada" (202). In Manrique's poem, the semion in question is composed of the signifier "vuestra poesya" (which references Poeta since it is his poetry in question), and the signified "señales . . . coloradas," which recalls the anti-Jewish legislation that required Jews to wear emblems that distinguished them from Christians. The implication of this association of terms is that Poeta is more like a Jew than a Christian because of his "distinctive emblem," that is, his Jewish lineage.

Anonymous poems, whose inclusion in sixteenth-century *cancioneros* suggests that they were composed during the second half of the 1400s, also contain semions. According to one, "Otra de un galán a Juan Poeta embiando le un sayo con un judío," a Jew is better suited to deliver a garment ("sayo") sent by the author because Poeta and the Jew speak the same language ("mejor entendáys"):[16]

> Este sayo vos embio
> en tal punto lo vistáys
> que del gozéys
> y lleuaos lo este judío
> porque mejor entendáys
> . . . .
> más pues soys de vn linage
> él judío y vos marrano
> entenderéys su lenguaje. (*Segunda parte* 195)

The allegation made by the anonymous author, that Poeta is able to communicate with the "judío," carries with it the inference that Poeta is accustomed to dealing with Jews, which could form the basis for charging *conversos* with heresy before the Inquisition. This might appear to suggest that the poem dates from after 1480, although it is, of course, impossible to speak with such precision regarding the work's composition. In any case, the parallel between the poet's allegation and one of a number of trivial delations that could incriminate *conversos* regardless of whether they were actually heretics reflects the contemporary perception that lineage determined one's status as a Christian.

The stigma of a Jewish lineage is imposed on Poeta in a semion located in the verse "él judío y vos marrano": the term "marrano," a signifier that references Poeta, is associated with the signified "judío" in a context that devalues Poeta's Christian identity. Poeta is entrusted with delivering the "sayo" because, as a "marrano" or inferior Jewish Christian, he communicates (in Hebrew? Ladino?) with the "judío" more effectively than the author, apparently because the latter does not share the same "linage." In this perpetuation of the image of the alienated *converso*, it is Poeta's "linage," regardless of his actual religious practices (which are not mentioned), that links him to the "judío."

A similar allusion is created in another anonymous work, "Otra copla de un cavallero a Juan Poeta porque Alegre, el Albardán, venía a la corte, do él estava":

> No os pesará, Juan, hermano,
> con Alegre, yo lo fío;
> no lo digo porque es frío,
> mas porque el fino marrano
> es la caxa del judío;
> y aunque ell'uno sea el dorado,
> entramos sois de un metal,
> siendo vos, Juan, el traslado
> y Alegre ell'original,
> no podés quereros mal. (*Cancionero de obras* 157)

The author of this poem evokes the image of an inferior Christian by underscoring a direct bond between Poeta, here the subject of the signifier "marrano," and the signified "caxa del judío." The inability of *conversos* to dissociate themselves from their Jewish roots is underscored by the term "caxa." According to the poet this is an entity that, even when adorned by a precious substance ("dorado"), retains its base identity ("metal"). By extension, the "marrano," treated as the "caxa del judío," retains his inferior (Jewish) identity even though he is a Christian.

Finally, the anonymous work discussed at the beginning of this chapter ("Otra a Juan Poeta hecha por un cauallero") includes a verse, "poeta juan tarabí" (*Segunda parte* 188), that may contain another semion. It is interesting to speculate that the word "tarabí" might actually be an erroneous transcription of "tarasí," meaning tailor, a signified that complements the reference to Poeta's circumcision by alluding to a profession that involves the cutting of materials. By extension, the association of "tarasí" with its signifier, "poeta juan," reinforces the allusion to circumcision in this poem that I identified previously.

The semions employed in the poems heretofore considered are formed by correlations between signifiers that denote a Christian entity (either Poeta or Montoro, or both of them) and signifieds that allude in various ways to Judaism or that recall the inferior condition of the *conversos*. In each case the associative total is the notion of a Jewish Christian, a metaphor for the socioreligious alienation of the *conversos*. To review, these semions are composed of the following signifiers and signifieds:

"A Juan de Valladolid" (Antón de Montoro), c. 1455

Signifier	Signified
vos y yo (Poeta and Montoro)	judíos

"Respuesta de Juan de Valladolid," c. 1455

Signifier	Signified
Malicioso desigual (Montoro)	judío

"Respuesta de Gómez Manrrique a Juan Poeta," c. 1460

Signifier	Signified
marrano (Poeta)	no judío ni cristiano

"Coplas del conde de Paredes ... en una perdonança en Valencia," c. 1470 (Rodrigo Manrique)

Signifier	Signified
Christian objects	Jewish objects
(Poeta's presence causes these objects to transform)	
bula del Padre Santo	escritura del Talmud
hierro	bezerro
bulto de la Señora	Tora
cáliz	cuchillo para vos circuncidar
patena	caçuela con berenjena
ara	ataifor con adafina
vos (Poeta)	rabí

"Coplas de Ribera ... Nápoles," early 1470s (Suero de Ribera)

Signifier	Signified
hijo (Poeta)	cristiano o de la ley de Mosén
él (Poeta's nephew)	judío
nieto (Poeta's nephew)	quemado
mujer (the wife of "nieto")	presa
Antón de Montoro	nariz

"Coplas del conde de Paredes ... Fez," not before 1476 (Pedro Manrique)

Signifier	Signified
prisión (Poeta's captivity)	poder de faraón
os (Poeta)	hijos de Abraham
vos (Poeta)	judío
Poeta (the implied subject)	Yahudí

"Otras trobas de Gómez Manrrique," c. 1476
 Signifier   *Signified*
 vos (Poeta)   nouicio, confeso
 mayor (Poeta)   delos ebreos
 Trobador (Poeta)   syn capirote
"Coplas de Gómez Manrrique a Johan Poeta," second half of the fifteenth
 century (?)
 Signifier   *Signified*
 vuestra poesya (Poeta's verses)   señales . . . coloradas
"Otra de un galán" (anon.), second half of the fifteenth century (?)
 Signifier   *Signified*
 marrano (Poeta)   judío
"Otra copla de un cavallero" (anon.), second half of the fifteenth century (?)
 Signifier   *Signified*
 marrano (Poeta)   caxa del judío
"Otra a Juan Poeta hecha por un caballero" (anon.), second half of the
 fifteenth century (?)
 Signifier   *Signified*
 poeta juan   tarasí (?) (another allusion to
                                      circumcision?)

Among the works that I examine in this book, those that involve Juan
Poeta present a unique inflection of the *converso* code. According to my
suggested chronology, this corpus of works spans the greatest time frame
of any I consider, thus allowing for some tentative assessments concerning
the significance of the *converso* code with respect to the evolution of anti-
converso discrimination during the second half of the fifteenth century. At
first glance, it appears reasonable to speculate that the semions in works
composed by the Manriques and Suero de Ribera are grounded in the animosity felt by these Old Christians toward *conversos*. Scholberg considers
and rejects this possibility in his evaluaton of the poems by the Manriques
and the anonymous works that I analyzed previously:

En primer lugar, son de carácter fuertemente personalista; atacan
cómicamente a una sola persona y no a todos los conversos. Son
invectivas, pero su propósito es burlarse de Juan Poeta y no el causarle
daño. Siguen en la misma tradición que forma los insultos que com-
pusieron trovadores contra juglares en épocas anteriores. Se basan,
pues, en el desprecio, real o fingido, del poeta de rango social superior
hacia el inferior. (343)

[In the first place, they are of a strongly personalized nature; they comically attack one person and not all *conversos*. They are invectives, but their intent is to poke fun at Juan Poeta and not to cause him harm. They follow in the same tradition of insults composed by troubadours who attacked minstrels in earlier times. They are grounded, then, in the real or feigned disdain felt by the poet of superior social rank for the inferior one.]

Moreover, as Scholberg observes (344), the insults launched by Old Christians are similar to those made by Montoro, a *converso*. Gómez Manrique's apparent enmity is also contradicted by his intervention on behalf of the *conversos* in 1484, when he helped to postpone the establishment of the Inquisition in Toledo until the following year (Paz y Melia xxiv–xxv). At the same time, in the case of Ribera, who has been labeled anti-*converso* (Scholberg 349), the employment of semions may reflect a hostility toward New Christians. Whether or not these Old Christian poets actually considered *conversos* to be inferior Christians, the language they used is similar in tone to the discriminatory discourse of the purity-of-blood statutes and Espina's *Fortalitum*. In other words, these Old Christians continued a medieval poetic tradition by exploiting discourse that reflects a contemporary reality, that is, the existence of a socioreligious distinction between Old and New Christians.

Merrell postulates that symbolic interpretations of literature are grounded in "culturally shared sets of experiences" (15). Regardless of whether it is grounded in actual animosity and regardless of whether it appears in an Old Christian or a *converso* text, the prevalence of the *converso* code demonstrates Merrell's premise by consistently depicting the image of the alienated *converso*. In addition, there is evidence suggesting that the semions that propagate this image parallel the historical evolution of anti-*converso* discrimination. This appears to be true in the cases of the previously discussed semions in Ribera's "Coplas de Ribera," which appear to deal with punishments meted out by the Inquisition. My analysis now delves further into this theme by exploring inflections of the *converso* code in works composed by New Christians during the successive stages of their socioreligious alienation.

Converso Literature
and Early Castilian Humanism

In postcolonialist thought the marginal voice of minority discourse strives to retain its individuality by defying a majority that seeks an elimination of cultural differences. Bhabha asserts that the essence of this discourse derives from the desire of a minority to legitimize its marginal position within a society.[1] By affirming and validating the factors that have engendered cultural differences, the discourse of a minority group attempts to subvert notions of cultural or historical superiority, not necessarily to dispel them but in order to renegotiate and retain its cultural identity. If we consider the postcolonialist conception of the marginal voice as one end of a spectrum, an example of the other extreme may well be found in the beginnings of the modern nation. For while the postcolonialist marginal voice accentuates its cultural differences in order to avoid assimilation, the relationship between the *conversos* and fifteenth-century Castilian humanism epitomizes the struggle faced by a minority that wished to merge seamlessly with a majority that sought to maintain social disparities in order to prevent assimilation.

In spite of the efforts of some scholars to deny the importance or refute the existence of humanism in Castile during the fifteenth century,[2] the activities of Diego de Burgos, Alonso de Cartagena, Juan de Mena, Alfonso Ortiz, Fernán Pérez de Guzmán, and the Marqués de Santillana, to name a few, clearly indicate that, although there were differences when compared to the movement in Italy, emergent humanism did establish a significant presence in fifteenth-century Castilian letters and thought.[3] With regard to the character of humanism during its infancy in Castile, one of the most misunderstood features is the moral facet of the movement.[4] The key to understanding the scope and significance of this current of humanistic thought may well lie in the tension between the expression by *conversos* of humanistic ideas stressing social and religious harmony and their difficulty integrating into an Old Christian society that had come to resent their conversion to Christianity. Scholars have touched upon this issue on several occasions.[5] What remains to be fully explored is the extent to which certain themes associated with early Castilian humanism—including conceptions of true virtue, honor, and nobility, and a desire for a Christian reformation based on the principles of the Church Fathers—influenced *converso* authors who, in turn, expressed them in literary works in reaction to their deteriorating social position.

Whether he had an indirect or direct influence on these authors, Alonso de Cartagena laid the ideological foundation for this trend in treatises that expressed humanistic ideals. Among the most prominent was the notion that true virtue and honor derived from moral character rather than lineage. Cartagena had expressed this notion as early as 1436, in his *Discurso:* "La noblesa natural consiste en la virtud moral, e según ésta, quanto alguno es más virtuoso de moral virtud, tanto es más noble" (208). Cartagena's espousal of this notion would become more pronounced in his best-known work, the *Defensorium unitatis christianae* (1450). The *Defensorium* was a platform for Cartagena to express his disdain for the two-tier Christianity that had been created by the Toledo rebellion of 1449.[6] In reaction to the discriminatory doctrines of the Sentencia-Estatuto (and those of the "Memorial" by García de Mora, which strove to justify that decree), Cartagena evokes a fundamental theological tenet in order to establish that the process of baptism erases a fortiori any distinction between sincere Christians:

> no hay que hacer diferencia alguna entre los fieles de si descienden de éste o del otro pueblo, cuando todos, al estar establecidos dentro de la fe católica, constituyen un pueblo único e indivisible. De aquí que no se pueda tolerar a aquellos que llaman a unos nuevos y a otros viejos, porque no existe católico alguno que no haya llegado a la fe recientemente, ni la virtud del agua bautismal pasa de uno a otro de modo que por el bautismo del padre nazca cristiano el hijo. Porque así como estando encerrado en el vientre de la madre nadie puede ser circuncidado, nadie tampoco estando encerrado en el vientre materno puede ser bautizado. De manera semejante si una mujer encinta es bautizada, el pequeño embrión que lleva en su vientre no queda bautizado. (*Defensorium* 206)

Cartagena's discussion of virtue is an extension of this argument in favor of equality among Christians. The theme is intertwined with his exploration of the nature of nobility, which had a special significance for *conversos* after the promulgation of the Sentencia-Estatuto. Although the Sentencia-Estatuto, like other purity-of-blood statutes, did not explicitly prevent *conversos* from entering the nobility (in fact, many nobles were from *converso* families), the possibility that purity of blood might eventually be used as a means of excluding *conversos* from this social stratum was a legitimate concern.

The extent to which this concern influenced *converso* thinking is reflected in Cartagena's affirmation of the eligibility of *conversos* for admission into the Christian nobility.[7] As Cartagena explains, this eligibility derives from their biblical heritage:

> Es de sobra sabido pues, que esta triple clase de nobleza [teológica, natural o moral, y civil] la han tenido muchos israelitas antes de su infidelidad, y tantas veces la Sagrada Escritura da testimonio de que algunos de ellos fueron agradables a los ojos de Dios, adquiriendo así la nobleza teológica, que no sería justo dudarlo. (*Defensorium* 320)

At the same time, only certain *conversos* are predisposed to achieve such status:

> ¿Cómo, pues, se puede dudar de que en aquel pueblo [judío] en el que hubo sacerdocio y reino hayan brillado algunos con el esplendor de la nobleza como en otras naciones? Lo que no quiere decir que llame nobles a todos los de aquel pueblo, sino que llamó nobles a algunos de sus individuos, como en otros pueblos, porque ni existió, ni existe nación alguna en la que todos sean nobles. (*Defensorium* 223)

Although Cartagena distinguishes between those who can be noble and those who cannot ("En los hombres, entre otras muchas, se ha establecido esta diferencia: que unos sean tenidos por nobles y otros por plebeyos" [*Defensorium* 282]), he clearly establishes the primacy of virtuous deeds in determining one's suitability to possess this attribute. In other words, while only those *conversos* of noble ancestry are deemed eligible to enter the Christian nobility, the only way to confirm this eligibility is by observation of their virtuous deeds, in particular their courage and skill at military pursuits:

> es lógico que conjeturemos que en algunos de ellos aquella nobleza poseída en la antigüedad haya estado oculta . . . al quedar purificada por la aceptación de la fe . . . se dispone de nuevo a lanzar sus rayos y esplendor porque estaba acostumbrada a difundir su luz. . . . Y este rescoldo [de nobleza], desaparecido el humo, vuelve a mostrar su luz,

y los pincha como con espuelas para que aspiren ardientemente a elevarse a los trabajos de la milicia, porque así como se dice, según el historiador escolástico, que el fuego del sacrificio en la época del cautiverio babilónico se había mantenido durante mucho tiempo enterrado, así se mantiene en la profundidad del corazón de los infieles un pequeño fuego de nobleza que empezará a brillar poco a poco una vez desechada la infidelidad.

De aquí que la Iglesia de Dios no pase en silencio la nobleza de aquellos, sino que volviendo al pasado la recuerde con nueva alegría.

. . .

Nadie, pues, juzgue como algo nuevo o desconocido, si abandonada la ceguera interna y recibida la luz interior de la verdad, los que hayan tenido esa nobleza, aunque obscurecida, la reciben ya clarificada. (*Defensorium* 285–86)

While maintaining a posture grounded in medieval feudalism, as in the *Discurso,* Cartagena expresses in this passage the humanistic concept that virtue supersedes lineage, contradicting the Sentencia-Estatuto while providing an ideological foundation for preventing future anti-*converso* discrimination.

Concern over whether purity of blood might restrict *conversos* from the nobility undoubtedly increased in the aftermath of the Toledo rebellion. The obvious relationship between increased anti-*converso* sentiment and the deterioration of royal authority produced a response by Cartagena, whose advocacy of a reformed monarchy in the *Defensorium* sprung from his *converso* status. In addition to being the bishop of Burgos, Cartagena was also very active in the govenment of Juan II.[8] Cartagena's political career exemplifies that of the fifteenth-century *converso* courtier who benefited from royal patronage within a Castilian society that was becoming increasingly anti-*converso.* Supporting the Castilian monarchy, even when a weak ruler occupied the throne, usually meant supporting the only ally in power the *conversos* possessed.

Because the monarchy was responsible for granting titles of nobility, the king's effectiveness was of special interest to *conversos,* who stood to lose the right to be named to the nobility if the concept of purity of blood were permitted to influence decisions regarding royal entitlements. This reformist attitude was common among humanists throughout Europe, with political ties (in addition to socioreligious designs, in Cartagena's case) often dictating whether a writer supported a republic or a monarchy. In this light, Cartagena depicts a fortified monarchy that is capable of establishing civic unity: "no puede existir gobierno, si no existe potestad de mandar, y de administrar justicia. . . . Y esta potestad procede del mismo rey. . . . Y como esta voluntad, expresa o tácita, de Vuestra Majestad no se da, la plebe . . . según el derecho no alcanza el nombre de ciudad y se queda bajo el nombre de (la) turba o plebe o muchedumbre de gentes" (*Defensorium* 395).

Diego de Valera's *Espejo de verdadera nobleza* was composed around two years after the *Defensorium*.[9] Whereas Cartagena approaches the nature of nobility from a theological perspective, a reflection of his clerical vocation, Valera, whose entrance into the royal court was facilitated by his father's position as physician to Juan II, "shift[s] Cartagena's emphasis away from theology and scripture toward a notion of the existence of civil and temporal nobility which cogently vindicates the *conversos'* social place and secular courtly aspirations" (Gerli, "Performing Nobility" 23). Notwithstanding the difference in their perspectives, both *conversos* underscore the role of the monarchy in determining nobility, a theme that is evident in Valera's assertion "que si alguno por mill años virtuossamente biviese y el príncipe mucho lo amase, que siempre quedaría popular e plebeo, hasta que por el príncipe le sea dada alguna dignidad o nobleza por la qual aya diferencia entre él y los plebeos" (*Espejo* 95).[10]

While both the *Defensorium* and the *Espejo* were responses to the discriminatory provisions of the Sentencia-Estatuto, there is reason to believe that Valera was also motivated by King Juan II's decision to sanction the statute in 1451. Valera may have interpreted the king's decision as a potential threat to the future ability of the *conversos* to enter the ranks of the nobility. This hypothesis might explain some of Valera's assertions regarding the qualifications for nobility, such as: "los nobles siguiendo virtudes llegasen al fin de la soberana nobleza, e los que menos son nobles o ninguna cosa, nuevamente serlo pudiesen" (*Espejo* 89). In the latter group Valera includes those who are not currently noble but who might attain nobility "si algo de bien escriviese podiese ser actorizado, aprovado e publicado" (*Espejo* 89), the inference being that an impartial and authoritative ruler is paramount in the granting of noble titles. Implicit in Valera's assertion is the worry that such impartiality might not exist, which would suggest that he was inspired by a desire to articulate to Juan II, to whom the work was dedicated, that discrimination based on lineage should not bias the authority who bestowed nobility.

In the *Espejo*, Valera parallels Cartagena by asserting that honor (and, by extension, nobility) springs from virtue: "Con todo esto ay algunas cosas por las quales los príncipes se mueven o deven mover a dar las dignidades . . . ca por los actos virtuosos se deven dar las dignidades, segunt pone Aristótiles . . . que el honor es galardón de la virtud, y por ende sólo a los virtuosos deve ser dado" (93). Valera also echoes Cartagena by applying these principles to the *conversos*. He begins by declaring that nobility transcends religious affiliation: "los convertidos a nuestra Fe, que segunt su ley o seta eran nobles . . . no solamente . . . retienen la nobleza o fidalguía después de convertidos, antes digo que la acrescientan" (*Espejo* 102). Valera then argues that it would be unjust to deny honor to virtuous (and sincerely Christian) *conversos*, whose adoption of the Christian faith should erase the stigma of their lineage:

> E como quiera que el judío o el moro segunt su ley o seta puedan virtuosamente bevir, las virtudes a los no bautizados no pueden tanto valer que por ellas ganen la theologal nobleza. E si así fuese que los que segunt su ley o seta seyendo nobles convertidos a nuestra Fe perdiessen la nobleza, seguir y a que no oviese diferencia entre pecar e usar de virtud: pues como a la virtud sea devido galardón e al pecado pena, a los tales sería dada pena en lugar de galardón, lo qual sería contra toda egualidad e justicia, la qual no dexa mal sin pena ni bien sin galardón. Pues de necesidad se sigue, que los tales venidos a la verdadera Fe, no solamente retengan la nobleza de su linaje, antes la acrescienten tanto que honestamente bivieren sin se entremeter en viles oficios ni venir a malas costunbres . . . e así el santo baptismo dado en significación de la santa pasión suya, lava e quita todos los pecados pasados así como si fechos no fuesen. (*Espejo* 103)

Valera further supports the inclusion of virtuous *conversos* within the nobility by reminding "los ignorantes [que] piensan el contrario" (*Espejo* 103) that these *conversos* descend from a noble lineage: "Ca si de la nobleza de los judíos abtoridades queremos, muchos podemos fallar, ca escripto es en el quarto capítulo del Deuteronomio, onde fablando de los judíos dize: '¿quál es otra nasción así noble?'" (*Espejo* 103). As Valera explains, according to Christian tenets the act of sincere conversion confers noble status on those who had possessed it previously: "éstos, convertidos al verdadero conoscimiento, son restituídos e retornados en el grado que en su principio . . . lo qual se prueva por aquellas palabras de nuestro Señor. . . . E pruévase asimesmo por abtoridad de Sant Gregorio" (*Espejo* 103–4).

Cartagena's *Defensorium* and Valera's *Espejo* were composed at a time when Juan II afforded the *conversos* some measure of royal protection. As the relationship between the *conversos* and the monarchy deteriorated during the reign of Enrique IV, humanistic ideals were perpetuated by a group of writers who included *conversos* such as Juan Álvarez Gato, Rodrigo Cota, and Pero Guillén de Segovia (also known as Pero Guillén de Sevilla).[11] This group has come to be known as the literary circle of the archbishop of Toledo, Alfonso Carrillo, and is thought to have formed around 1460 under the auspices of Carrillo, who served as archbishop in the years 1446–82. An Old Christian himself, Carrillo worked to achieve equality between Old and New Christians and to provide a sanctuary for a wide range of individuals, including those of his literary circle.[12] Fernando del Pulgar says of him:

> Tenía en su casa letrados e caballeros e ommes de fación.[13] Rescibía muy bien e honraba mucho a los que a él venían, e tratábalos con buena gracia, e mandábales dar gran abundancia de manjares de diversas maneras, de los cuales fazía siempre tener su casa muy proveída, e tenía para ellos los oficiales e ministros necesarios e deleitábase en ello. (111)[14]

Carrillo's patronage helped to ensure that the circle flourished through the chaotic years of the 1460s and early 1470s, until it finally ceased to exist around 1474 (Moreno Hernández, *Pero Guillén* 33). The intellectual climate within the circle, exemplified by Carrillo's own concerns for both warlike and intellectual pursuits ("Era gran trabajador en las cosas de la guerra. . . . Plazíale saber esperiencias e propriedades de aguas e de yerbas, e otros secretos de natura" [Pulgar 112]),[15] encouraged the participation of "letrados e caballeros e ommes de fación" (Pulgar 111) such as Gómez Manrique, who shared Carrillo's kind disposition toward the *conversos*, and whose diverse exploits, typifying those of the *caballero letrado*, were esteemed by *conversos* in the group. An appreciation for those humanistic qualities commonly associated with the figure of the *caballero letrado* is found in the "Proemio" to *La gaya ciencia*, in which Pero Guillén de Segovia lauds Carrillo's military prowess during the social disturbance of 1467 along with his intellectual interests ("vuestro claro ingenio y loable voluntad todavia vos inçita . . . a leer las dotrynas de los antiguos filosofos y sabios" [43]). The same notion is incorporated into two poems in which Juan Álvarez Gato attributes these qualities to Hernán Mexía ("Para el mismo Hernán Mexía . . . porque era muy leydo y muy sabio en todo" and "Queriéndose partir Hernán Mexía a su tierra" [Artiles 121–24]).

It was in such a climate that humanistic ideas advocating the elimination of distinctions between Old and New Christians were disseminated among *conversos*, who, in turn, saw them as ideological justification for a reform of the social and political practices contributing to their alienation. This quest for social harmony is expressed at times through semions that speak to the ideals articulated by Cartagena and Valera, ideals that gained an increased significance as anti-*converso* sentiment intensified during the middle of the fifteenth century. Each of these semions consists of a signifier that references an individual *converso* or the *conversos* in general and a signified that expresses how *conversos* might be accepted as Christians according to humanistic ideals. By advancing these ideals, the semions allude to the alienation of the *conversos* by contradicting the attitudes that relegated them to an inferior socioreligious status.

Some *conversos* affiliated with Carrillo's circle apparently responded to the contemporary desire for Church reform so that all Christians might be treated as equals. This Pauline attitude was a likely reaction to the papal retraction of the punishment meted out to the perpetrators of the Toledo rebellion, which appeared to contradict Rome's condemnation of the Sentencia-Estatuto, and the discriminatory ideas advanced in Espina's *Fortalitium* a decade later. Indeed, members of the Old Christian clergy also felt repugnance at the affront to Christian dogmas that the Sentencia-Estatuto represented. For example, two years after Cartagena composed the *Defensorium*, Fray Lope de Barrientos dedicated a brief treatise to King Juan II entitled "Contra algunos zizañadores de la nación de los conuertidos del pueblo de Israel." Barrientos refuted the provisions of the Sentencia-Estatuto, which he called "muy gran blasfemia" (185), on the grounds that they opposed the teachings of the Church:

> E guardarse hía en aquesto muy poco el honor a Ntro. Señor Jesucristo, si por uenir a la fé los que son de aquella línea de su santa Humanidad, quedasen infamados y deshechados y sin honras ni beneficios. ¡Qué tan grande error sería en la fé nuestra, si lo tal así pasase[!] . . . E que [pereciese] el santo bautismo e eficacia de él, el cual hace al baptizado *nueuo home*, e laua e quita del todo la culpa e pecado. (185–86)

Cartagena had advanced a similar notion in the *Defensorium*, in which he pointed out that no theological distinction should exist between Old and New Christians:

> En Cristo, pues . . . se disipó toda la ceguera de los ojos del corazón de una y otra gente, y cesó toda diferencia de pueblos y de linages,

porque todos volvieron en este segundo Adan puro a la unicísima unidad. . . . Y esto vuelve a significar Pablo con doctrina de autoridad apostólica en otro lugar presentándolo de una manera especial y con diferentes palabras [Gal. 3.27–28]: "cuantos en Cristo habéis sido bautizados, os habéis vestido de Cristo. No hay ya judío o griego, no hay siervo o libre, no hay varón o hembra, porque todos sois uno en Cristo Jesús." (135)

Valera had also argued against discrimination on theological grounds:

¿quién es que non sepa ser todos venidos de aquel solo primero padre Adam, e la fe o creencia aver fecho apartamiento entre las nasciones que después vinieron? E pues todos de aquella una raís somos produzidos, ¿quién dubda no ser mejores los que un Dios solo sirvieron e honrraron que aquellos que falsos dioses creyeron e adoraron? Por los quales—conviene saber por los gentiles—el Apóstol, A los romanos, en el capítulo onzeno, desía: Tú, como fueses oliva montesina non convenible para buen fruto, eres enxerida de los ramos firmes de la pura oliva; conviene saber, de los judios convertidos, de los quales la Iglesia fue fundada segunt paresce por aquellas palabras de nuestro Señor, que dixo: "Tú eres Pedro, y sobre aquesta piedra la mi Iglesia fundaré." (*Espejo* 104–5)

Among the writers of Carrillo's circle, these precepts had a special meaning since lineage was the tinder for the intensification of anti-*converso* discrimination. An example of Pauline humanism is found in a poem by Álvarez Gato. According to the rubric, the work was written while Álvarez Gato was situated "Al pie dun cruçifiçio questa en Medina sobre vna pared hecha de huesos de defuntos" (Artiles 136). This highlights the backdrop against which his discourse strives to illustrate that all Christians are equal, as the rubric continues: "puso esta copla para que veamos claramente cómo somos duna masa" (Artiles 136).[16] The semion in this rubric is found in Álvarez Gato's declaration "somos duna masa." The word "somos," which alludes to both Old and New Christians, functions as a signifier, and "duna masa" is a signified that evokes the Pauline ideal (in a theological sense given that it is avowed "Al pie dun cruçifiçio"). The association of these terms constitutes an expression of the egalitarianism with which *conversos* (and Old Christians) advocated Church reform. The text of Álvarez Gato's poem is replete with this ardor for religious harmony:

> Tú, que miras todos estos,
> piensa, pecador de ty,
> que diformes y dispuestos
> de buenos y malos gestos
> de todos estan aquí;
> y pues son duna color
> el sieruo con su señor,
> yo te consejo que mires
> en ser en vida mejor
> y ni penes ni sospires
> por ser mayor y menor. (Artiles 136)

In these lines the words "todos," another signifier that designates Old and New Christians, and "duna color," a signified that once more articulates the Pauline ideal, are linked again in support of egalitarian Church reform.

A lengthy poem by Guillén, "Señor, oye mis gemidos," communicates this egalitarianism through an impassioned plea directed to God: "Señor, oye mis gemidos / y rogarias / . . . / inclina las tus orejas a mi clamor" (Azáceta 173). According to Guillén, an acceptance of this humanistic principle would permit an escape from an unjust monarchy, "la monarchía / de crueles" (Azáceta 190), a likely reference to the complicity of Enrique IV in the intensification of anti-*converso* discrimination. Guillén implores the Almighty to eliminate the differences between Old and New Christians, "Señor Dios, tú clarifica / desiguales" (Azáceta 174); stresses unity, "Poder, querer y saber / en unidad" (Azáceta 176); and envisions a harmonious existence among all Christians who live by the tenets of their faith:

> Todos cuantos nascerán
> y son nascidos,
> con servicios elegidos
> te servirán;
> desde 'l pobre con afán
> hasta el rey,
> tus mandamientos y ley
> guardarán. (Azáceta 196)

In a passage found earlier in the poem, "Cría en mí, por tu mesura, / coraçón / muy limpio" (Azáceta 189), Guillén expresses this Pauline ideal by means of a semion. The signifier "coraçon," which references Guillén's spiritual identity, is linked to the signified "limpio," a term that alludes to the religious purity inherently possessed by Old Christians. The associative total of this correlation, a metaphor for religious equality among Old and New Christians, speaks to an idyllic coexistence to which *conversos* undoubtedly aspired. In the context of a contrary social reality, this metaphor reflects on the marginal status of the *conversos*.

The humanistic primacy lent to character, an idea grounded in the Stoicism of Seneca and perpetuated by Cartagena and Valera,[17] had a special appeal for the *conversos* since it implied that any virtuous individual merited equal treatment as a Christian. Among the writers of Carrillo's circle, this theme is reflected in two "Proemios" as well as in poetry. In one "Proemio," which serves as an introduction to *La gaya ciencia*, a treatise on poetry, Guillén incorporates the theme into his discussion of nobility. While reviewing the "grandes y notables fechos" (39) of Carrillo, Guillén pauses to establish that only virtuous deeds (here in battle) are capable of endowing an individual with the quality of nobility:

> Y tanto quanto el onbre es mas claro y noble tanto deue tener mayor cuydado de la virtud y tener que las herydas rresçebidas en tan justas causas son señales de gran nobleza; de que se sigue que mucho mejor es la nobleza que se gana con tales peligros y se saca de tan asperos lugares, que la que se dexa por heredat a los subçesores. (41)

A little further on Guillén extends his elaboration to include true honor, which, like nobility, derives from virtuous deeds:

> Varon es el que de la honrra cura, porque en las cosas humanas ninguna otra cosa paresçe mas digna que la honrra, porques don de gloria al que la rresçibe. Y ninguna cosa se compra por mayor presçio que aquella que por galardon de virtud se gana. . . . Y Tulio dize en su libro De ofiçios que . . . la onestad mas se judga por verdaderas obras que por bozes del pueblo. (42)

In his "Proemio," Álvarez Gato, after citing Seneca, asserts that virtue alone should determine the quality of an individual's character:

> pues que buenos nos deseamos, como concuerda Seneca, avnque sin lunbre de fe, syno guiado de buena razón y de amigo de la virtud, en el primero libro de la *Bienauenturada vida*, do dize: "No cato yo los onbres por el color de las vestiduras con que traen cubiertos los cuerpos, ni los juzgo con los ojos corporales, pues tengo otra mas çierta lunbre para apartar lo bueno de lo falso". . . . En conclusion, lo

que defiendo y digo es que do quiera que la bondad o qualquiera
virtud se halle, ally se mire y ally se honrre. (Artiles 166–67)

On two occasions Álvarez Gato expressed this theme through semions.
In the rubric to the previously discussed work, "Al pie dun cruçifiçio," the
poet declares "y que éssos deuen ser auidos por mejores, que touieren más
virtudes" (Artiles 136). The semion in this passage consists of "éssos," a
signifier that references the *conversos* since they too might be included
among those considered "mejores," this term being a signified that alludes
to the achievement of such status by the possession of "más virtudes." The
correlation that Álvarez Gato creates between these terms evokes the social inferiority of the *conversos* by dissociating the attribute of being
"mejor" from genealogy, which is ephemeral, as the rubric avows: "pues
que linaje, dispusiçión y fama y rriquezas todo pereçe" (Artiles 136). By
underscoring this humanistic theme Álvarez Gato attempts to establish
that *conversos* should be included among the "mejores" regardless of lineage, which countered the ideology imposed by the purity-of-blood statutes.

In another poem, with a lengthy rubric that begins "Vn moço despuelas
de Alonso de Velasco que se llamava Mondragón hizo çiertas coplas de
loores bien hechas al capitán Hernán Mexía de Jaén y a Juan Áluarez,"
Álvarez Gato informs the reader that he will speak to the world out of
sheer frustration over the contemporary appreciation of virtue: "Habla
con el mundo çerca duna condiçión de gran culpa nuestra que tenemos de
pregonar virtud del grande o del rrico, avnque no la tenga" (Artiles 105).[18]
The subsequent verses illustrate his concern that the virtuous characters of
individuals fail to distinguish them:

¡Oh mundo desordenado,
abundoso de ynvirtud!
¿Cual rrazon nos da cuydado
que juzgemos por estado
la bondad ny la virtud? (Artiles 105)

Further on in the poem, Álvarez Gato emphasizes that such virtue derives
from good deeds, regardless of wealth:

Sy virtudes son halladas
en el pobre y en el chico,
que sigamos sus pisadas,
que se loen y sean loadas

> por ygual cal rrico, rrico.
> Y sy asy tenprado fuere,
> no sera menester freno;
> tengala quien la tuuiere,
> sy mejor obra hiziere
> ayanle por el más bueno. (Artiles 105–6)

In the rubric to the passage that follows, Álvarez Gato discloses his motivation for composing this work:

> Trae a consequencia aquel pobre rropero de Córdoua, Antón de Montoro . . . que fue la causa destas coplas, diziendo que sy éstos obraren o hablaren bien, o otros generalmente, no les deue enpachar beuir en ábito baxo o pobremente para ser oydos o loados. (Artiles 106)

The declaration in the rubric that individuals should not be encumbered by inferior spirituality ("no les deue enpachar beuir ábito baxo") is undoubtedly an allusion to the religious status of the *conversos,* which again voices the social egalitarianism advocated by *conversos* in Carrillo's circle. Álvarez Gato continues the poem by expressing this theme in semionic terms:

> No hagamos Dios del oro,
> dexemos este aguaducho;
> sy bien obra el de Montoro,
> avnque pobre de tesoro,
> ténganle por rrico mucho[.] (Artiles 106)

In the semion in question, "Montoro" is a signifier that references a *converso* and "rrico" a signified that designates how Montoro should be treated according to an egalitarian ideal. The reference to Montoro's impoverished economic state ("avnque pobre de tesoro") situates him on an equal plane with the "pobre" mentioned earlier, who deserves to be esteemed "por ygual cal rrico" with regard to virtue. As an extension of the poem's central theme, that any worthy individual should be considered virtuous, Montoro, in spite of his lineage, deserves to be wealthy in terms of virtue ("ténganle por rrico mucho") as determined by the moral quality of his actions ("sy bien obra el de Montoro").

Cota and Guillén also addressed this theme in poetry. Although neither poet employs semions, their works are significant in the present context for the manner by which they combine discussions of virtue with the humanistic desire for monarchic reform that undoubtedly intensified among *conversos* as the 1460s progressed. The two poems in question are thought to have been composed around 1470 (Moreno Hernández, *Pero Guillén* 54), that is, after years of intensified anti-*converso* persecution for which the king was to some extent responsible. Against this historical backdrop, Cota composed a "Respuesta" in response to a "Pregunta" by Gómez Manrique concerning whether *caballeros* existed before *reyes*. In his "Respuesta," Cota displays a preoccupation for a type of nobility that is based in virtue rather than lineage:

> que ser noble en quanto ser
> recto rey nin voluntario
> no da don tan esencial
> por muy excelsa grandeza,
> nin la vngnata vileza[19]
> alinpia el çetro real. (*Cancionero castellano* 105)

In these lines Cota argues that virtue is above lineage, that there is a moral order above the social order. Despite lineage one can and should be held ethically accountable. According to Cota, the existence of true nobility depends on the actions of the individual and *reyes* cannot create the quality of nobility. In his poem, *caballeros* existed before *reyes*: "caualleros auie quando / vinieron reyes rigiendo" (*Cancionero castellano* 105). Nevertheless, *reyes* are essential if *caballeros* are to have their titles.

In Cota's poem it is the royal ability to assume preeminence over the *caballeros* that enables the system to function:

> mas tal nombre cauallero
> si por la horden se dixese,
> presupone rey que fuero
> al tal título pussiese. (*Cancionero castellano* 105)

While *reyes* are responsible for establishing control over their *caballeros*, the social position of those who ostensibly possess such authority does not necessarily imply individual merit. In other words, the status of being noble or royal does not, by itself, constitute authority: "no da don tan esencial." Implicit in Cota's poem is the notion that a monarch must earn the right to rule (needless to say, by his just and virtuous actions), an honor that Enrique IV clearly did not merit during the 1460s.

Guillén entered into the debate by composing "Otra respuesta alas mesmas de Gómez Manrrique, fechas por Pero Guillén de Seuilla, atrauesada." Like Cota, Guillén implies that genuine nobility ultimately derives from an individual's character, rather than from his title:

> Como no puede boluer
> vn metal en su contrario,
> porque en su primero ser
> quedara de neçesario,
> así no puede vileza
> gozar de sangre real,
> ni menos poca firmeza
> cobrar nonbre de real. (*Cancionero castellano* 106)

In a contemporary social context, it is likely that the propositions of Guillén and Cota would have been embraced by most, if not all, *conversos*. Like Church reform, their humanistic desire for a reformed monarchy undoubtedly stemmed from dissatisfaction with the complicity of Enrique IV in the social alienation of the *conversos*.

The *conversos'* embrace and diffusion of humanistic ideas appeared to support ideologically their assimilation into the majority. In poems in which semions appear, recognition of the potential for this assimilation is evident in the associations of signifiers and signifieds that advocate that all Christians be beneficiaries of egalitarian Christian doctrines:

"Al pie dun cruçifiçio questa en Medina" (Álvarez Gato)

Signifier	Signified
somos	duna masa
todos	duna color
éssos	mejores

"Señor, oye mis gemidos" (Guillén)

Signifier	Signified
coraçón (Guillén's spiritual identity)	limpio

"Vn moço despuelas de Alonso de Velasco" (Álvarez Gato)

Signifier	Signified
Montoro	rrico

It might have altered the course of the relationship between Old and New Christians if the humanistic ideas espoused by the *conversos*, in the works by Álvarez Gato and Guillén and those that do not display semions, had been incorporated into mainstream thought. For example, had King Enrique IV adopted the reformist doctrines advocated by the *conversos* of

Carrillo's circle rather than the discriminatory ideas advanced in Espina's *Fortalitium,* anti-*converso* persecution may have stopped at the local level.

Against the backdrop of the postcolonialist conception of the marginal voice of minority discourse, which attempts to avert assimilation by asserting its individuality in the face of a majority that wishes to maintain homogeneity, it is ironic that the marginal voice of the *converso* minority, which disseminated humanistic ideas in order to disavow its individuality and achieve assimilation and legitimacy, ultimately failed. Instead, the *conversos'* espousal of a cultural agenda that was compatible with Old Christian ideals contributed on an ideological plane to the birth of modern Spain. While Old Christian authors and rulers embraced the humanistic ideas disseminated by the *converso* writers of Carrillo's circle, the incorporation of these ideas into mainstream Spanish thought never resulted in the acceptance of the *conversos* as equal Christians. Thus it was that *conversos* advanced Spanish culture as a whole by perpetuating a current of heterogeneity, albeit in a nation that was to become impaired by its own religious homogeneity.

The Deification of Queen Isabel the Catholic in *Converso* Poetry

The dissipation of Carrillo's circle coincided with an end to the most perilous period of the reign of King Enrique IV. The pogroms of the 1460s and early 1470s concluded more than a decade of relative stability following the Toledo rebellion of 1449. As I discussed in Chapter 1, the onset of these pogroms signified that anti-*converso* persecution had become national in scope, in part due to royal collusion. After the relative tranquility of the 1450s, King Enrique IV's discriminatory policies, including the adoption of ideas advanced in Espina's *Fortalitium*, expedited the nationalization of this phenomenon. In the preceding chapter, I examined the culturally motivated response to the charged atmosphere of the 1460s and early 1470s. Concurrent to this response, *converso* writers also expressed their dissatisfaction with the political situation by openly attacking King Enrique IV. This *converso* literary reaction served as a prelude to the subsequent stage in the evolution of the *converso* code. Because of the optimism generated by the ascension to the throne in 1474 of Queen Isabel the Catholic, several *conversos*, including those who had criticized King Enrique IV, drastically changed their deprecatory attitude toward the monarchy. These *conversos* depict the new queen as a divine figure capable of alleviating social tensions. The *converso* tendency to deify the queen is found in poems composed between 1474 and 1480, when it appeared that she was working to improve relations between Old and New Christians.

During the reign of King Enrique IV, assaults on the monarchy were also made by Old Christians such as Gómez Manrique and Hernán Mexía, and in anonymous works such as "Coplas de Mingo Revulgo" (which may have been written by a *converso*).[1] However, *converso* works are unique in being specifically inspired by events that precipitated the decline of the New Christians. These socially motivated attacks on the king are found in both literary and nonliterary works. An example of the latter is an epistle composed by Diego de Valera in 1462 ("Otra epístola suya que al señor rey Don Enrique enbió"), in which Valera lists several reasons for the dissatisfaction of Castilians with the current monarch. The fifth item on the list refers indirectly to the escalation of anti-*converso* persecution during the early 1460s: "quinta, e no menos principal, que todos los pueblos a vos sujetos, reclaman a Dios demandando justicia como non la fallen en la tierra vuestra" ("Epístolas" 8). Valera's assertion that "todos los pueblos" are not receiving fair treatment undoubtedly alludes to the 1462 uprising against the *conversos* of Carmona and the king's failure to mete out punishments for the atrocities committed. It should be pointed out that the intensity of the uprising of 1462, which initiated the wave of pogroms during the 1460s and early 1470s, had not been equaled since the Toledo rebellion of 1449, as Alonso de Palencia underscores:

> haré mención del levantamiento que concitó contra los conversos, a quienes tuvo por más hacedero entregar a las iras de la facciosa conjuración de los malvados, sedientos de sus riquezas, al apellido de religión; cual si ésta mandase el saqueo, el asesinato y la violenta perpetración de todo género de infamias, como lo habían hecho antes en Toledo, y como lo hicieron después los ladrones siguiendo el pernicioso ejemplo. (136)

The Carmona uprising was concurrent to the king's adoption of an anti-*converso* posture. The year before he had called for a papal bull in an attempt to establish a Castilian Inquisition. After the violence in Carmona, he was unwilling to protect the *conversos* (partly out of deference to Don Beltrán de la Cueva) and instead helped to foment anti-*converso* sentiment, as Palencia explains:

> Terrible y criminal fue el tumulto de Carmona, y bien hubiera necesitado rápido remedio; más como D. Enrique no quiso ponerle por consideración a D. Beltrán de la Cueva, que era hermano del alcaide Beltrán de Pareja, se echó mano de subterfugios para aparentar cierta manera de castigo, el cual consistió en que saliese cierto Diego de Osorio, que se llamaba corregidor, con tropas de Córdoba y Écija y algunas de Sevilla, a contener algún tanto a los revoltosos, que no a entregar a cada uno lo suyo, según la verdadera definición de la justicia. Este inícuo proceder fue causa de nuevas desdichas que, como explicaré, padece sin interrupción en la villa de Carmona. (136)

In his epistle, Valera recognizes the king's complicity in the eruption of violence. Immediately after he admonishes the king for permitting unjust conditions to exist ("todos los pueblos . . . demandando justicia como non la fallen en la tierra vuestra" ["Epístolas 8"]), Valera declares that the public officials he empowers are making the problem worse:

> E disen que como los corregidores sean hordenados para faser justicia e dar a cada uno lo que suyo es, que los más de los que oy tales oficios exercen son onbres inprudentes, escandalosos, robadores e cochadores,[2] e tales que vuestra justicia venden públicamente por dinero, sin temor de Dios ni vuestro; e aun de los que más blasfeman es, que en algunas cibdades e villas de vuestros reinos, vos, Señor, mandáis poner corregidores no los aviendo menester, nin siendo por ellos demandados, lo qual es contra las leyes de vuestros reinos. ("Epístolas" 8)

Attacks leveled in *converso* poetry also demonstrate hostility toward King Enrique IV. In response to the anti-*converso* riot of 1474 in Carmona, Antón de Montoro dedicated a poem to the king ("Montoro al rey nuestro señor sobre el robo que se hizo en Carmona") in which he begs him to bring the Old Christian perpetrators to justice and protect the *conversos*. Montoro opens his work with a frustrated cry protesting the actions of a monarch who has permitted the *conversos* to become frequent objects of persecution:

> si fablo con osadía
> es por ver de cada día
> lo que dixo Salomón;
> si quisierdes perdonarme
> seguiréis la vía usada,
> e si a pena condenarme,
> ¿qué muerte podéis vos darme
> que ya no tenga pasada? (Ciceri 296)

Further on Montoro provides an account of the tragedy on behalf of his fellow *conversos*, who, in addition to having been exposed to physical violence, had their property ransacked:

> Viérades a los señores
> ser sujetos, y sus bienes;
> viérades a los dadores
> ser esclavos pedidores

y sus bidas en rehenes;
como quando lidian toros,
¡o rey de gran exçelencia!
tomándoles sus thesoros,
que en los más crueles moros
se hallará más clemençia. (Ciceri 299)

Montoro implores the king to come to the aid of the *conversos* several
times in the poem. However, the last stanza displays his frustration at the
futility of directing his plea toward a monarch seen as ineffectual in con-
taining anti-*converso* violence:

Ansí que, rey liberal,
quien nunca supo dar buelta
en lid temida canpal,
en este vasallo tal
es de fazer a man suelta;
a tal hombre son anejos
bienes, pues tan bien alterca
obrando contra los quexos:
quien así os sirve de lexos
deçid, ¿qué fará de zerca?
    E si tan sin yntrevalos
como su gentil familia
fuesen todos,
pocos escándalos malos
terníamos en Castilla
destos modos. (Ciceri 301)

In the same remonstrative spirit, Juan Álvarez Gato composed a poem
("Al tienpo que fue herrido Pedrarias por mandado del rrey don Enrrique,
pareçió muy mal porque era muy notorio que le fue gran seruidor . . . y
algunos caualleros . . . se despidieron del rrey") in reaction to an event that
typified the king's discriminatory attitude toward the *conversos*. The work
was inspired by the king's incarceration of the *converso* Pedro Arias Dávila
(Pedrarias), a *contador mayor* and Álvarez Gato's employer and friend.
Pedrarias had been accused of stealing money from the royal treasury, an
unfounded accusation that caused Pedrarias and Álvarez Gato to side with
Enrique's half-brother Alfonso, who appeared to have a much more favorable policy toward the *conversos*. The first three stanzas reflect Álvarez
Gato's disgust with the king:[3]

No me culpes en que parto
de tu parte,
que tu obra me desparte,
sy ma[l]parto;
que a los que me dieren culpa
en que partý,
yo daré en rrazón de my
que tu culpa me desculpa.
    Que cosa pareçe fuerte
de seguir,
quien rremunera seruir
dando muerte.
Yrse tan todos los buenos
a lo suyo,
queres brauo con el tuyo
y manso con los ajenos.
    Plázete de dar castigos
syn por qué:
no te terna nadie fe
de tus amigos.
Y essos que contigo están,
çierto so,
cuno a vno se tiran
descontentos como yo. (Artiles 96)

The literary animosity by *conversos* toward the monarchy changed after a shift in power occurred. The actions of Enrique's successor, Isabel,
during the years leading up to the official establishment of the Inquisition
in 1480, provided *converso* poets with the ideological foundation for the
uniquely positive manner in which they portrayed her. To be sure, both
Old and New Christian writers of the time depicted Isabel as a pillar of
strength and stability. However, in poems by *conversos* there is a unique
tendency to express confidence in the queen by endowing her with divine
attributes and, at times, by employing semions that praise her attempts to
unify the Christian community. Each of these semions consists of a signifier that evokes the poet's inclusion in a tragic experience and a signified
that endows Queen Isabel with the ability to end that tragedy. Inasmuch as
the poems that incorporate these semions were composed between 1474
and 1480, the years during which Isabel acted on behalf of the *conversos*,
the associations between these lexical items are reflections of the messian-

ism with which the queen was endowed. This attitude, present in *converso* poems that incorporate semions and in those that deify the queen without making recourse to such terms, is diametrically opposed to the manner by which the same authors treat Enrique IV, an ideological divergence that parallels the change in fortune for the *conversos*.

Poems by Fray Íñigo de Mendoza,[4] Diego de San Pedro, Montoro, Álvarez Gato, and Pedro de Cartagena[5] participate in this trend. Mendoza, a member of a religious order (the Franciscans) that persecuted the Jews,[6] may have become a "[f]erviente partidario" (Rodríguez Puértolas, *Poesía crítica* 218) of Queen Isabel because she advocated a reform of the religious orders. On two occasions he composed works that celebrate the beginning of an era of greater tolerance. The first is a lengthy panegyric to both of the Catholic Monarchs, "Coplas al muy alto y muy poderoso príncipe, rey y señor . . . E a la muy esclarescida reina doña Isabel," that was composed before 1479. The assignation of this date derives from the rubric, which designates Fernando as "príncipe de Aragón" (Rodríguez Puértolas, *Fray Íñigo* 318), a position he occupied until January 1479, when he became king of that region.[7] In this work Mendoza depicts Isabel as more celestial than human:

> Vos, reina, sois la figura
> quien deshaze nuestro mal;
> vuestra gentil hermosura
> fue pintada por pintura
> más divina que mortal;
> vuestra sabia juventud
> ya sobra para muger;
> vuestras obras son salud;
> . . . .
> Pues si, reina esclarescida
> Dios vos hizo en este modo,
> tan sin par y sin medida,
> para ser más escogida
> abéislo de ser en todo[.] (Rodríguez Puértolas, *Fray Íñigo* 331–32)

A semion in this passage contributes to Mendoza's glorification of the queen's divine abilities. A collective signifier, "nuestro mal," which refers to an adverse situation, is countered several lines below by the term "salud," a signified that expresses the rectification of "nuestro mal" by the queen ("vuestras obras"). The associative total of this correlation is a metaphor for Mendoza's confidence in Isabel's capacity for restoring order ("Vos, reina, sois la figura / quien deshaze") to a Castile that had been left, as the poem reads, "tan dañado" (Rodríguez Puértolas, *Fray Íñigo* 326) by Enrique IV.

Another poem by Mendoza, "Dechado a la muy escelente reina doña Isabel, nuestra soberana señora," appears to have been written around the same time as his "Coplas" for the queen, judging by the recentness of the injustices it describes, which were committed during the reign of Enrique IV:

> No piense vuestra excelencia
> que es clemencia
> perdonar la mala gente,
> antes de tal açidente
> comúnmente
> se causa la pestilencia;
> si no, ved por esperiencia
> qué presencia
> os demuestra vuestra tierra,
> que el no pugnir a quien yerra
> dio tal guerra
> a la real providencia
> qual vos muestra su dolencia.
>   Pues reina nuestra señora,
> lo que dora
> los reales gobernalles
> es que anden por las calles
> los firmalles
> desta espada matadora,
> pues ya la gente traidora,
> robadora,
> anda suelta sin castigo[.] (Rodríguez Puértolas, *Fray Íñigo* 284)

The allusion to "la gente traidora, / robadora, / [que] anda suelta sin castigo" explicitly recalls Enrique IV's negligence after the atrocities committed against the *conversos*. In contrast, Mendoza speaks of the queen as if she were the Virgin herself:

> Alta reina esclarecida,
> guarnecida
> de grandezas muy reales,

a remediar nuestros males
desiguales
por gracia de Dios venida,
como quando fue perdida
nuestra vida
por culpa de una muger,[8]
nos quiere Dios guarnecer
e rehacer
por aquel modo y medida
que llevó nuestra caída. (Rodríguez Puértolas, *Fray Íñigo* 281)

The divinity with which she is endowed confers on Isabel the power to "remediar nuestros males." Although this phrase does not contain terms that may be said to form a semion, it represents another collective reference that may be understood to voice a *converso*'s hope for an end to the persecution that had plagued the period of Enrique IV's reign.

The *converso* ancestry of Diego de San Pedro has been a topic of critical debate. Marcelino Menéndez Pelayo's theory that he was of *converso* ancestry appeared to be confirmed by Emilio Cotarelo, who claimed to have discovered historical proof.[9] Three decades later, Keith Whinnom ("Was Diego de San Pedro a *converso*?") cast doubt on some of Cotarelo's findings. However, while Whinnom challenges the familial relationships that Cotarelo endeavored to establish, he does not successfully refute the theory of San Pedro's *converso* origin.[10] Cotarelo focused on several sixteenth-century *pruebas de linaje,* investigations that were required for entrance into Spanish military orders, which did not admit *conversos.* Diego de San Pedro was identified as a *converso* on several occasions during these investigations. One witness indirectly identified him as such in testimony provided in Badajoz in 1569. This witness told of the time that he asked an elderly man about the lineage of Ana de Ulloa. The reply given by the elderly man enlists San Pedro as a member of a *converso* family: "que era hija de un Fulano San Pedro, hermano de Diego de San Pedro, un trovador, y que era confesa" (Cotarelo 323). In 1592, again in Badajoz, another witness said that "ubo quien avía dicho que doña Ana de Ulloa tenja una raza de cristiana nueva y que era por parte de su padre que se llamaba Pedro de San Pedro [*sic*], que compuso . . . un librillo que se intitulaba La Cárcel de Amor" (Whinnom, "Was Diego de San Pedro a *converso*?" 194).

Although the attribution of *Cárcel de amor* to Pedro de San Pedro is an obvious error, the testimony of 1592 is nevertheless significant inasmuch as a relationship is established between *Cárcel* and a *converso* author. In his introduction to *Tractado,* Whinnom mentions two more examples of testimony, given in Badajoz and Jerez de la Frontera in 1585, in which San Pedro was labeled a *converso* (San Pedro, *Obras I* 19). In sum, the repeated testimonial link between San Pedro and a *converso* lineage, and the fact that "San Pedro" was one of the most common surnames to appear on lists of *conversos* brought before the Toledan Inquisition in 1495 and 1497 (Cantera, *Judaizantes* xxxiii), both suggest that he was a New Christian.

Diego de San Pedro's *Tractado de amores de Arnalte y Lucenda* is thought to have been composed near the end of the 1470s.[11] *Tractado* has traditionally been appreciated for being the second Spanish sentimental novel, a genre that was initiated by Juan Rodríguez del Padrón in 1439. While the composition of *Tractado* signified a continuation of the genre, several features of the work suggest that San Pedro also incorporated a social theme that responded to the historical circumstances for *conversos* during the late 1470s. San Pedro announces this social theme in his dedication of the work to "las damas de la Reina" (*Tractado* 127):

> Pero vosotras, señoras, rescebid mi servicio, no lo que con dureza en el dezir publico, mas lo que con falta en el callar encubro, de manera que si los motes la obra sufriere, la voluntad las gracias resciba, agradesciendo no lo que dixere, mas lo que dezir quise. (*Tractado* 127)

San Pedro's supplication that his readers look beneath the surface of his plot is, I believe, a call to focus on an episode that culminates in a lengthy poem, "La más alta maravilla," in which Queen Isabel is again deified. At first glance this episode appears to be out of context in the work. It has nothing to do with the plot, which up to this point deals solely with the anguish of Arnalte, and it is followed by a phrase "Buelve la habla a las damas" (*Tractado* 138) that indicates that San Pedro considered the episode to be a digression. However, the placement of the episode at the beginning of the work, along with the tone of the poem dedicated to the queen, suggests a social motivation.

Apart from references in the dedication ("Sant Pedro a las damas de la Reina" [*Tractado* 127]) and the closing remarks ("Acábase este tratado llamado San Pedro a las damas de la reina" [*Tractado* 202]), the only mention of Isabel occurs when a despondent Arnalte briefly forgets his suffering by imploring the narrator, called auctor, for information regarding the queen:

> Y como para bien responder aparejado me viese, con demasiada tristeza començó a preguntarme, y . . . después de dezirme cómo al Rey nuestro señor conoscía e después de sus excelencias contarme,

por la Reina nuestra señora me preguntó, deseando saber si hombre
de manificencia tan grande igual compañía que le perteneciesse tenía.
(*Tractado* 132)

Arnalte's petition occurs after a mass has been celebrated, a backdrop that
enhances the subsequent depictions of the queen in "La más alta
maravilla" as an object of divine veneration:

> Porque yo con tan mal modo
> de hablar ¿qué diré d[e] ella?
> pues quien nos hizo de lodo
> tuvo con su saber todo
> muy bien que hazer en ella (*Tractado* 133);
> mas quísola Dios fazer
> por darnos a conoscer
> quién es Él, pues fizo a ella (*Tractado* 134);
> porque demos gloria a Él
> cuando miramos a ella (*Tractado* 136);
>   ¡Oh, cuántas vezes contemplo
> con qué dulces melodías
> ha de ir al eterno templo!
> según nos dize su enxiemplo
> ya después de largos días;
> y después que así la elijo,
> pienso con alma elevada
> en el gozo sin letijo
> que havrán la Madre y el Hijo
> con la huéspeda llegada. (*Tractado* 137)

San Pedro's vision of Isabel is intensified when "La más alta maravilla" is
considered as a component of a thematic parallel within *Tractado*. Such
parallelism, a common technique in late-medieval Spanish prose,[12] is revealed when "La más alta maravilla" is compared to the other long poem in
Tractado, "Invocación a Nuestra Señora," which appears at the end of the
work. The fact that *Tractado* opens with a deification of the queen and
closes with a poem in praise of the Virgin places these two women on the
same plane, underscoring the queen's divine attributes.

As in other *converso* poems that treat the queen in this manner, San
Pedro's depiction of Isabel stands in opposition to references to the chaotic
reign of her predecessor:

¡Cuánto daño estava estante,
cuánto mal iva adelante,
cuánto bien quedava atrás;
    cuánta voluntad dañada
en Castilla era venida,
cuánta injusticia mostrada,
cuánta cizaña sembrada,
cuánta discordia nascida! (*Tractado* 137)

In contrast, the queen is presented as a figure who restores order:

Es reina que nunca yerra,
es freno del desigual,
es gloria para la tierra,
es la paz de nuestra guerra,
es el bien de nuestro mal;
es igual a todas suertes
de gentes para sus quiebras,
es yugo para los fuertes,
es vida de nuestras muertes,
es luz de nuestras tiniebras. (*Tractado* 133–34)

These lines contain four semions that are typical of this stage of the *converso* code. Each contains a collective signifier ("nuestra guerra," "nuestro mal," "nuestras muertes," "nuestras tiniebras") that is rectified by its association to its antonymous signified ("paz," "bien," "vida," "luz," respectively), this association recalling the messianism with which Isabel was imbued.

The most graphic use of divine imagery occurs in Montoro's "Canción de Antón de Montoro en loor de la Reyna doña Ysabel de Castilla," which must have been written between 1474 and 1477, the year of his death. Once again, a *converso* poet's attitude toward Queen Isabel contradicts his treatment of King Enrique IV. By the time he had composed his poem to Enrique IV in 1474, Montoro had personally witnessed some of the worst anti-*converso* violence, and even may have been forced to flee his home in Córdoba in 1473, during a riot in which a number of *conversos* were killed (Ciceri 15). His plea to Enrique IV voices the frustration of the *converso* who has all but lost hope that the persecution will cease. In contrast, his poem dedicated to Isabel indicates that the new queen had restored in the poet some degree of optimism for the future. While Montoro invokes the notion of death in connection with Enrique IV ("¿qué muerte podéis vos darme / que ya no tenga pasada?" [Cicieri 296]), Isabel is associated with life and transformed into a divine being:

Alta Reyna soberana
si fuérades antes vos
que la hija de Sant'Ana,
de vos el Hijo de Dios
recibiera carne humana.

   Que bella, santa, discreta,
por espiriencia se prueve,
aquélla Virgen perfecta,
la divinidad ecepta,
esso le debéys que os deve.

   Y pues que por vos se gana
la vida y gloria de nos,
si no pariera Sant'Ana
hasta ser nascida vos,
de vos el Hijo de Dios
rescibiera carne humana. (Ciceri 219–20)

Unlike in those previously identified, a collective signifier does not inform the semion in this passage. At the same time, the notion of a collective benefit deriving from the queen's divinity is an outgrowth of the correlation between the signifier "Alta Reyna," which references Isabel, and the signified "Virgen perfecta." Due to the divine ability with which she is endowed, a particular group in which Montoro includes himself by using the first person plural pronoun ("nos"), stands to prosper ("la vida y gloria de nos").

Although it does not include a semion similar to those employed by Mendoza, San Pedro, and Montoro, a poem by Álvarez Gato, "Coplas de Juan Álvarez Gato a la Reyna nuestra Señora," must be mentioned for its participation in this literary trend. Álvarez Gato's revelation in the poem that he has recently begun his association with the royal court (which occurred during the late 1470s [Márquez Villanueva, *Investigaciones* 29–30]), "pues que a mi poco biuir / en respeto de os seruir" (Artiles 130), indicates that it is concurrent to the others under consideration. In sharp opposition to his bleak perspective on Enrique IV, Álvarez Gato depicts in this work the optimism felt by *conversos* during the early years of Queen Isabel's reign:

Vienen de todos lenguaxes,
bárbaros, loros, guineos,
turcos, armenios, hebreos,
alaraues y caldeos:
los muy rrobustos saluages.
. . . .

Danse gran prisa a venir
como quien ba por salud,
al son de vuestra virtud
viene tan gran multitud,
que quieren el sol cubrir.
Traen un bulliçio y meneo
ques cosa destremidad
y es la voz de su desseo
de ganar el jubileo
de mirar vuestra beldad. (Artiles 126)

Like his *converso* contemporaries, Álvarez Gato portrays the queen in a divine light:

De grandes loores digna,
la sagrada mano diestra
os hizo muy más veçina
a su Magestad diuina
que a la forma común nuestra.
Que aunque lo callase yo,
vuestro gesto es buen testigo
de la graçia que vos dio
y quanto se trauaxó
para ygualaros consigo. (Artiles 128)

To be sure, scholars have debated the identity of the "Reyna nuestra Señora" mentioned in the rubric. Márquez Villanueva attempts to identify the object of Álvarez Gato's veneration as Doña Juana, the wife of Enrique IV (*Investigaciones* 264). In response, R. O. Jones argues convincingly that Álvarez Gato's poem refers to Queen Isabel. According to Jones, the precise identity of Álvarez Gato's subject is revealed further on in the work:

Seis letras negras de amores
en mi coraçón sangriento
vi zarcadas de dolores,

que mostrauan las colores
que tiene mi pensamiento[.] (Artiles 129–30)

Jones explains that the "Seis letras" allude to the six letters that compose
the name "Isabel" (62). In support of his argument he points out that a
similar reference to the queen's name is found in "Otras suyas a la reyna
doña Ysabel," a poem composed by Pedro de Cartagena during the second
half of the 1470s (Jones 58, 63). Cartagena, whose allusion to the queen's
ability to impose her authority ("la .s. señorear / toda la tierra y el mar")
may have been inspired by the murder of his uncle during the attack on
the *conversos* in Toledo in 1467 (Avalle-Arce 294), lauds the queen by ex-
plaining that the letters in her name represent different attributes:

Que sea poco en la verdad
ser, reyna, vuestro renombre
oyga vuestra magestad
daré por auctoridad
las seys letras de su nombre
que la .y. denota imperio
la .s. señorear
toda la tierra y la mar
y la .a. alto misterio
q[ue] no se dexa tocar.
    Y la .b.e.l. dizen
lo natural no compuesto
que[n] vuestra alteza está puesto
ellas no se contradizen. (*Cancionero general* lxxxvii)

Although, like Álvarez Gato, Cartagena does not include a socially motivated semion, his deification of the queen echoes the attitude of the other
converso poets considered in this chapter:

De otras reynas difere[n]te
princesa reyna y señora
[¿]q[ué]smalte porne q[ue] assiente
enla gra[n]deza excelente
q[ue] con su mano dios dora[?]
. . . .
    Una cosa es de notar
q[ue] mucho tarde contesce
hazer q[ue] temer y amar

esten juntos sin rifar
por q[ue]sto a dios pertenesce[.] (*Cancionero general* lxxxvii)

The existence of a corpus of *converso* poetry dating from the period 1474–80 in which Isabel is consistently deified,[13] and the lack of contemporary Old Christian examples that portray Isabel in this manner, suggest that the *converso* poems share a common motivation. This motivation becomes clear when it is recalled that this technique is employed by the same *converso* poets who had reflected on the precarious nature of their social situation during Enrique's reign. With respect to all of the poems heretofore considered, it is reasonable to conclude that the *conversos* who deified Isabel utilized poetry as a vehicle for communicating the hopes they felt until 1480, the year that the papal bull establishing an Inquisition finally went into effect.[14] In the cases of the poems that incorporate semions, the frequent recourse to collective signifiers (or an indirect reference to collectiveness in Montoro's poem) indicates an awareness of a shared experience, that is, the nationalization of anti-*converso* persecution during the 1460s and early 1470s:

"Coplas . . . a la . . . reina doña Isabel" (Mendoza)

Signifier	Signified
nuestro mal	salud

"La más alta maravilla" (San Pedro)

Signifier	Signified
nuestra guerra	paz
nuestro mal	bien
nuestras muertes	vida
nuestras tinieblas	luz

"Canción . . . en loor de la Reyna" (Montoro)

Signifier	Signified
Alta Reyna	Virgen perfecta

The importance for all *conversos* of the ascension to the throne of Queen Isabel, a monarch whose actions in favor of the *conversos* might have helped end more than a decade of anti-*converso* uprisings, is reflected in the nature of these correlations. To be sure, the semion in Montoro's poem does not explicitly refer to a collective tragedy. However, his attitude voices the optimism shared by *conversos* during the queen's first years in power, an optimism whose magnitude is underscored by the ideological divergence between works dedicated to the queen and those directed to her predecessor.

In a broader sense, the pro-Isabelline attitude of the *converso* poems that deify Isabel situates them within the "preponderance of pro-feminist literature" (Ornstein 15) composed in fifteenth-century Spain.[15] At the same time, the sociopolitical nature of the *converso* poems sets them apart from the vast majority of contemporary Spanish pro-feminist compositions. While these works tend to praise women in general terms—by extolling feminine attributes (such as beauty and chastity), advocating respect and admiration of women in general, enumerating the biographies of virtuous women of the past in order to underscore feminine virtue, and so on—the *converso* works considered in this chapter were not meant to defend all women. They were written because the urgency of their author's social predicament and the past failures of the monarchy called for an appeal to the new monarch, who appeared to represent a change for the better, urging that she act on behalf of the *conversos*. Even when the language of these works is couched in the rhetoric frequently used in *cancionero* poetry to "reconciliar, asociar y equiparar el amor humano con el amor de Dios" (reconcile, associate, and equate human love with the love of God [Gerli, "La 'religión del amor'" 66]), the social dimension of their deifications of the queen distinguishes them from "la enorme cosecha de poemas sacro-profanos de los cancioneros" (the enormous collection of sacro-profane poems in the songbooks [Gerli, "La 'religión del amor'" 69]) and bonds them thematically by a unique social optimism.

When she became queen of Castile in 1474, Isabel the Catholic achieved true authority over her kingdom, something that few other contemporary women were able to accomplish. As Margaret King observes, "Most women in the ruling classes [of the Renaissance] did not rule, but only shared some of the prerogatives of sovereignty. In the vibrant artistic and intellectual climate of the Renaissance . . . this meant that they exercised the power of patronage" (160). Of course, Isabel (as King mentions) did actively participate in the intellectual development of the early Spanish Renaissance. However, as a ruler she was much more than a patron and actively pursued objectives that were to shape the course of Spanish history. One of these, the religious unification of Spain, led to the establishment of the Inquisition, an event that brought to a close the brief period during which the queen appeared to be working toward resolving the social conflicts between Old and New Christians. In the end, the figure once depicted as if she were the Virgin herself ultimately acted to ostracize the *conversos* even further and to ensure that they would be perpetual targets of discrimination.

Rodrigo Cota's "Diálogo entre el Amor y un Viejo"

A *Converso* Lament

Rodrigo Cota's "Diálogo entre el Amor y un Viejo" is a poem that debates whether the flames of passion can counteract the sensorial deprivation that inevitably comes with the passing of time. Even on this superficial level "Diálogo" may be considered an allegorical work. Amor and Viejo, the characters who personify the abstract concepts of Love and Old Age, engage in a disputation that has a universal normative significance. Viejo, at first skeptical, is eventually enticed by Amor into attempting to recapture the ardor of his youth, only to find that his age makes this impossible. Viejo is ultimately rejected and abandoned by Amor and ends the poem by lamenting his foolish decision, an allusion to the folly of aspiring to contradict the laws of nature. My objective in this chapter is to read Cota's poem in a different sense, that is, as allegorically alluding to anti-*converso* persecution in general and the particular manner by which Cota was affected.

Semiotic, semionic, and allegoric analyses share a common feature: in each case, the validity of meaning depends on the consistency with which interpretive standards are applied. This is a notion implicit in many definitions of allegory, such as the one provided by Northrop Frye in *Anatomy of Criticism:*

> We have actual allegory when a poet explicitly indicates the relationship of his images to examples and precepts, and so tries to indicate how a commentary on him should proceed. A writer is being allegorical whenever it is clear that he is saying "by this I *also* (*allos*) mean that." If this seems to be done continuously, we may say, cautiously, that what he is writing "is" an allegory. . . . But even continuous allegory is still a structure of images, not of disguised ideas, and commentary has to proceed with it exactly as it does with all other litera-

ture, trying to see what precepts and examples are suggested by the imagery as a whole. (90)

Without mentioning semiotics or semionics, which did not become popular methods of literary interpretation until after the publication of *Anatomy of Criticism*, Frye indirectly underscores a link between these methods and allegoric interpretation in his avowal that the meaning of allegory is derived by "trying to see what precepts and examples are suggested by the imagery as a whole." In other words, allegoric interpretation also imposes upon the critic the responsibility of formulating a methodology that is only valid insofar as it is uniformly applied. Just as valid semionic interpretation, as I underscored in Chapter 2, depends on the repeated applicability of the norms with which it is implemented, an interpreter must consistently follow the same criteria in judging whether the "continuous" presence of "examples" and "precepts" informs a text with allegorical meaning.

In order to provide a foundation for allegoric interpretation, the reader should be able to distinguish between levels of meaning. This concept is crucial because some works may be understood allegorically on more than one level. Moreover, the revelation of one allegorical meaning does not exclude the revelation of another. Distinct allegories can coexist in the same work and the presence of different levels of meaning only implies that they are different, not that one is more valid than the other. A cursory look at Juan de Mena's *Laberinto de fortuna* serves to illustrate this point. On one level, Mena's poem contains allegorical allusions that speak to the mutability of fortune in a general sense. For example, the stanzas dedicated to perpetuating the tragic fate of Macías (st. cv–cviii) might be said to contain an allegorical lesson that could apply to any individual who thinks of involving himself in the "fuego viçioso de illícito amor" (st. cix). At the same time, if the poem is considered in a contemporary political light, the allegorical meaning takes on a new dimension as a reflection of what John Cummins calls "la época laberíntica en que se escribió" (the moral atmosphere of a nation . . . consumed by fraternal conflicts) (Mena 27), the allegorical meaning takes on a new dimension as a reflection of "el ambiente moral de la nación . . . que se consume en luchas fratricidas" (Mena 29).

Multiple allegories also coexist in "Diálogo." In addition to the "surface" allegory, two parallel socially motivated allegories beneath the surface recall the contemporary social status of the *conversos*. The existence of this social dimension to Cota's poem has been suggested on several occasions. The first to discuss "Diálogo" in this context was Castro, who circumscribes the poem as an example of

la tradición sombría . . . de conversos desesperados, sin cómodo
asiento en este mundo. . . . Recuérdese la perversa complacencia de
Rodrigo de Cota al incitar al Viejo de su célebre *Diálogo* a rendirse a
la llamada del Amor, para, inmediatamente, confrontar al hombre
anciano con las miserias de su edad, con la "desrealidad" de su sueño.
(*La realidad* 534–35)

[the somber tradition . . . of desperate *conversos*, without a comfort-
able place in this world. . . . Consider the perverse complacency of
Rodrigo de Cota upon inducing Viejo in his renowned *Diálogo* to sur-
render to the call of Amor, whereupon the old man is immediately
confronted with the miseries of his age, with the "disreality" of his
dream.]

Elisa Aragone again touches upon the relationship between the tone of the
poem and Cota's social status as a *converso:* "Rodrigo Cota era, come
sappiamo, un *converso:* la concezione pessimistica dell'amore, già tipica di
tanta trattatistica medievale, si esaspera con biblica violenza nel semita
ispano" (Rodrigo Cota was, as we know, a *converso:* the pessimistic conception of love, already typical in many medieval treatises, is intensified [in
his poem] with a brutal [tone of] biblical [proportions common in works
by] Hispanic Semites) (Cota 25). In his discussion of the *converso* use of
the topos of old age, Márquez Villanueva makes a similar comment:

Como puede apreciarse, los conversos manifiestan un decidido apego
a la discusión literaria de la vejez, aunque no muestran, fuera de su
curiosidad por el tema y la general orientación desengañada, una
mayor identidad de puntos de vista, pues los dispersan sobre un
triángulo cuyos vértices son la alabanza impregnada de ascetismo
estoico-paulino (Álvarez Gato), la negación sarcástica, "positivista,"
de aquélla (Pulgar) y el negro pesimismo integral de Rodrigo de Cota.
(*Investigaciones* 310)[1]

[As can be seen, *conversos* manifest a decided fondness for literary
discussions of old age, although they do not demonstrate, apart from
their curiosity about the subject and a general attitude of disenchant-
ment, any greater commonality in points of view, which are dispersed
over a triangle whose vertices are praise tempered by stoic-Pauline
asceticism (Álvarez Gato), the sarcastic and positivist denial of the
other one (Pulgar), and the dark integral pessimism of Rodrigo de
Cota.]

Apart from these references, studies dedicated to analyzing the features of *converso* literature have neglected to provide a more elaborate commentary on the possible *converso* meaning of Cota's poem.[2]

What has been lacking is a situation of "Diálogo" in its sociohistoric context. Cota's life during the turbulent second half of the fifteenth century appears to have exemplified that of the *converso* who tried to assimilate yet found his attempts thwarted by an increasingly hostile Old Christian society. While he was still very young, Cota personally experienced the event that initiated systematized anti-*converso* persecution. His father, Alonso, was a victim of the anti-*converso* riot of 1449, during which the family home was set on fire (Benito Ruano, *Toledo* 35), and several members of the Cota family are mentioned in the Sentencia-Estatuto.[3] Thus from an early age Cota would have realized that *conversos* could be targeted for economic motives regardless of their religious practices. After the riot of 1449, the Cota family continued to be the object of persecution and discrimination. Only a few years after the establishment of the Spanish Inquisition, the Holy Office tragically affected the Cota family when Dr. Alonso Cota, the poet's first cousin, was burned at the stake in 1486 for Judaizing.[4] An *escribano* named Juan Cota is on a list of individuals brought before the Inquisition in 1492 and 1493 (Fita 319).[5] Two lists of Judaizers from 1495 and 1497 mention fourteen Cotas (including Dr. Cota) as *condenados, habilitados,* or *reconciliados,* or as children of those who were in some sort of trouble.[6] Among the latter were the poet's nephew Sancho, the son of Dr. Cota, and another first cousin, Rodrigo.

Perhaps the most startling aspect of the poet's life concerns his personal involvement with the Inquisition. Although there is no evidence that suggests that Cota was ever a crypto-Jew, near the end of his life he was brought before the tribunal and listed as a *condenado*. A reference to this inquisitional action is found in a royal decree dated September 30, 1499:

> Los Reyes Católicos dan poder a Fernand Rodríguez del Varco y al licenciado Fernando de Mazuecos, inquisidor en Toledo y a Francisco de Vargas, receptor de los bienes confiscados para que hagan composición con los herederos de Sancho de Toledo, por unas casas que hubo comprado de Rodrigo de Cota y que pertenecían al fisco por haber sido este condenado.[7]

Although the outcome of Cota's case has yet to be determined, the effect that it appears to have had on his children suggests that, even if he was acquitted before being required to appear in an auto-de-fé, the fact that he had been accused at all caused irreparable damage to the family name. José Gómez-Menor observes that, in 1526, two of the poet's sons, Martín de Alarcón and Juan de Sandoval, "ya omitían cuidadosamente el apellido Cota al referirse a su padre, a quien designan con el nombre de *Ruy Sánches de Toledo*" (now carefully omitted the surname Cota upon referring to their father, whom they designate by the name *Ruy Sánches de Toledo*) (149).[8] The omission of the surname from an official document is a possible indication that his sons were attempting to hide their relationship to an individual who had been listed as a *condenado*.

The two men may have felt compelled to hide the surname Cota because both the Holy Office and civil authorities "prohibieron ciertos cargos honrosos a los descendientes inmediatos de los condenados por la Inquisición" (barred certain honorable posts to immediate descendants of those who had been condemned by the Inquisition) (Domínguez Ortiz, *Los judeoconversos en la España moderna* 137). In her study of *converso* families in Toledo, Linda Martz comments on the situation faced by those who, like Cota's sons, desired to distance themselves from a *condenado:* "after 1485 many Toledo conversos had reasons to seek a new identity. Many achieved this by changing their surname, whether adopting a new one or modifying the old one, and by attempting to disassociate themselves, at least publicly, from their forebears" (121–22). The fear of being linked to a *condenado* had existed ever since 1484, when Tomás de Torquemada issued a decree stating that descendants (including children and grandchildren) of *condenados* would be restricted from virtually all public offices. Later on, in 1501, the Catholic Monarchs barred the children of *condenados* from other professions (Kamen, *The Spanish Inquisition* 120–21).

It is, of course, impossible to know whether Cota was unjustly accused of heresy, that is, whether he was in fact a sincere Christian. However, as I underscored previously, anti-*converso* persecution was often unrelated to the religious practices of individuals and instead sprung from a general conviction that *conversos* were inherently inferior. A poem by Montoro, "Del mismo a unas que hizo Rodrigo Cota de Maguaque,"[9] reinforces this point with regard to Cota. In this work, which could not have been composed before 1474,[10] Montoro portrays Cota as a *converso* who attempts to act like a good Christian: "y assí queréis de troyano, / por hazer de muy cristiano" (Ciceri 167). In spite of being "muy cristiano," Cota is disenfranchised because of his Jewish heritage, according to Montoro's poem:

dexad las caballerías
y tomad la vara y peso,
que, graçioso y bien criado,
de muy garrido conpás,
quando muy mejor armado
y mejor encavalgado,
vos dicen: ñafee detrás. (Ciceri 170)

Montoro's appeal that Cota abandon "las caballerías" is a form of asking him to refrain from behaving like an Old Christian inasmuch as pure lineage, an attribute that only Old Christians were able to possess, was a prerequisite for becoming a *caballero*.[11] The term "ñafee" is a shortened form of "añafee" (a term used further on in the poem "de aquel papel añafee" [Ciceri 172]), an allusion to the document used to prove one's conversion to Christianity and a derogatory way of referring to *conversos* (Scholberg 324, note 33). In these lines Montoro reminds Cota that he cannot dissociate himself from his lineage. Although he practices the customs of the Old Christian *caballero* ("quando muy mejor armado / y mejor encavalgado"), Cota is called a *converso* behind his back ("vos dizen: ñafee detrás"). Once again, it should be noted that the extent to which this textual depiction of Cota is grounded in reality is unknown. However, regardless of whether Cota actually behaved like an Old Christian *caballero*, the predicament Montoro describes recalls that faced by *conversos* in general, who were assigned a collective genealogical stigma that haunted those who attempted to assimilate.

While a knowledge of Cota's biography is not essential to understanding the *converso* meaning of "Diálogo," it complements this interpretation of his poem. I submit that Cota's lifelong embroilment in anti-*converso* persecution enhances the possibility that "Diálogo" was influenced by his cognizance of his inferior socioreligious status. Among the *conversos* I examine in this book, Cota's case is unique because he suffered, both directly and indirectly, from the most varied forms of persecution.

My analysis of "Diálogo" will require the elaboration of a unique type of allegory that I call a *converso* lament, a manifestation of the *converso* code that reflects the intensification of anti-*converso* discrimination toward the end of the fifteenth century. In a *converso* lament I detect a certain pessimism, aggravated by a heightened social and political awareness, that expresses the author's frustration at his social position as a New

Christian and his protest directed at those who have forced him to go through life as an outcast.

A *converso* lament is a mode of literary expression common to oppressed individuals who, as Leo Strauss asserts, tend to produce "a peculiar type of literature in which the truth about all crucial things is presented exclusively between the lines" (in Nepaulsingh 6). As a reflection of the intensification of anti-*converso* persecution after the establishment of the Inquisition, the semions in a *converso* lament are allegorical allusions. While semions in *converso* works composed prior to 1480 speak to the *converso* condition in terms that are relatively explicit, *converso* laments tend to be more oblique, perhaps as a reflection of the social environment in which they were written. Although *converso* writers were not yet restricted by inquisitional censorship, which did not begin until 1551, the need to conceal social themes in literature undoubtedly became more pressing after 1480, when *conversos* began to be punished for any number of "heretical" activities. In Cota's case, the fact that during the first years of its existence the Inquisition in his native city of Toledo operated with unparalleled efficiency also suggests that fear of (further) persecution may have been the factor that induced him to veil the *converso* meaning of his poem.[12]

Because they are couched within an allegorical framework, the semions that inform "Diálogo," as in the two *converso* laments I analyze in the following chapter, recall the alienation of the *conversos* more indirectly than those that I have previously considered. These indirect semions are participants in the *converso* code for the manner by which they may be consistently assigned meaning according to the same criteria. Each will consist of a signifier, either a collective reference to the *conversos* or an individualized allusion to Cota himself, that is linked to a signified that defines different facets of the condition of being inferior. The associative total of each of these correlations will be seen to allude to the social decline of the *conversos* during the early decades of the Inquisition.

When "Diálogo" is considered as a *converso* lament, the presence of two parallel *converso* allegories is revealed: one, a macro-allegory alluding to the situation of the *conversos* in general, and the other a micro-allegory inspired in Cota's own circumstances. On the macro-level it should be understood that the somber theme of "Diálogo" is a re-creation of the social decline experienced by *conversos* during the second half of the fifteenth century. The character called Viejo symbolizes a *converso* who has suffered this decline, while the character called Amor represents a superior Old

Christian. The micro-allegory, while having its roots in the same social situation, specifically reflects the persecution experienced by Cota, who is also symbolized by Viejo.

The poem begins with Viejo situated in his orchard, which has lost its once flourishing beauty, as he relates in his first discourse directed to Amor:

> Quanto más qu'este vergel
> no produce locas flores,
> ni los frutos y dulçores
> que solíes hallar en él.
> Sus verduras y hollajes
> y delicados frutales
> hechos son todos salvajes
> convertidos en linajes
> de natíos de eriales. (Cota v. 10–18)

In the macro-allegorical context, the orchard, a symbol of life, is intended to symbolize the lives of the *conversos*. The particular reference to the *converso* predicament during the late fifteenth century is made by a semion composed of the signifiers "verduras" and "hollajes," which reference a former prosperity, and the signified "linajes de natíos de eriales," meaning barren wasteland and, by extension, implying an inferior condition that is incapable of flourishing. The link between these components is created by a term, "convertidos," that situates the allusion in a contemporary context. The "verduras" and "hollajes" of Viejo's orchard are converted into "linajes de natíos de eriales" just as a *converso* genealogy became an inferior stigma after the advent of systematized persecution. This metaphorical allusion to the dismal social situation of the *conversos* is enhanced as Viejo continues to bewail the dilapidated state of his orchard:

> La beldad deste jardín
> ya no temo que la halles,
> ni las ordenadas calles
> ni los muros de jazmín.
> Ni los arroyos corrientes
> de bivas aguas notables,
> ni las alvercas, ni fuentes,
> ni las aves produzientes
> los cantos tan consolables. (Cota v. 19–27)

To review, the central allusion in Cota's macro-allegory is created in his portrayal of Viejo as a subjugated individual whose orchard has become a wilderness. As a metaphor for a predicament faced by many *conversos*, Viejo's condition recalls the inferior socioreligious condition by which *conversos* came to be defined by the late 1400s. By that time, like Viejo's once-flourishing orchard, any early hope that anti-*converso* persecution might not become a nationalized phenomenon was a distant memory.

As the macro-allegory continues, the *converso* meaning of "Diálogo" becomes more apparent. Viejo is at first cautious and attempts to dissuade Amor from intruding into his orchard. Despite the efforts of Viejo, Amor chooses to remain and seeks to convince Viejo of his ability to bestow upon him that which he is lacking in his old age:

> Escucha, padre señor,
> que por mal trocaré bienes,
> por ultrajes y desdenes
> quiero darte gran honor. (Cota v. 109–12)

Amor's pledge to instill honor in Viejo ("quiero darte gran honor") should be understood in an ironic sense. By the sixteenth century, an individual's honor was determined by public perception and was an attribute reserved for those with pure Christian genealogies (Castro, *De la edad conflictiva* 73, 81). In these lines, the Old Christian (represented by Amor) is taunting the *converso* (represented by Viejo) by pretending that the *converso* can have honor; but because he is held in low public esteem, the *converso* is incapable of possessing honor.

As a component of a semion in the passage above, the term "honor" serves as a signified that is linked to two signifiers, "ultrajes" and "desdenes," which denote negative characteristics. The associative total of this correlation among antithetical concepts is a metaphor that makes an ironic jab at the social vulnerability of the *conversos*. Although not in terms that may be classified as semions, this theme resonates on other occasions in the poem. Further on, Amor directs a declaration at Viejo, "Donde mora este maldito / no jamás hay alegría, / ni honor, ni cortesía" (Cota v. 217–19), which mocks him by suggesting his lack of honor. Since Viejo is a representation of a *converso*, his cry of "¡deshonra vivos y muertos[!]" (Cota v. 173) communicates the same theme from a different perspective. *Conversos*, typified by the writers of the Carrillo salon (to which Cota belonged), had a conception of honor that stressed the value of individual deeds rather than lineage. According to the standards by which honor came to be bestowed, the *converso* could only live in "deshonra" due to his lineage, a frustrating situation recalled by Viejo's cry.

A few lines below, Viejo's words once again serve to announce the presence of the *converso*: "tú nos sabes enxerir / como egibcio nuestra vista" (Cota v. 179–80). In this passage, the semion consists of a signifier, "nuestra vista," which collectively alludes to the *conversos*, and the signified "egibcio" (meaning Egyptian), which recalls the suffering of the biblical Jews while in Egypt. By evoking this Old Testament episode, that is, by claiming that Amor encumbers ("enxerir") Viejo just as the Egyptians had encumbered the Jews, Cota draws a parallel between anti-*converso* and anti-Jewish persecution. This parallel is validated not only by the fact that *conversos* were treated as Jews but also in the similarity between the fate of the biblical Jews and the fifteenth-century *conversos*. In the Old Testament, Egypt is first seen in Genesis as a place of refuge for the Jewish people, who twice migrate there in times of famine (12.10, 46.6). During their second sojourn the Jews achieve great prominence due to the efforts of Joseph, who is named governor of Egypt (Gen. 41.40–42). However, the good fortune of the Jewish people eventually fades, and in Exodus they are reduced to slaves in a country where they once prospered.

As a *converso* who had lived (in pre-1492 Toledo) in proximity to a large Sephardic community, Cota may have been aware that the commemoration of the harsh years of slavery in Egypt had long been an integral part of Judaic tradition. He also may have known that the depiction of Egyptians as persecutors of the Jewish people is central to the festival of Passover, which occurs each spring in order to recall the difficult times in Egypt and the release from bondage. The Haggadah, the prayer book for Passover, has numerous references to the suffering of the Jews in Egypt. For example, concerning the Passover tradition of eating bitter herbs, the Passover Haggadah says: "They are eaten to recall that the Egyptians embittered the lives of our forefathers in Egypt" (23). Cota takes the Old Testament reference and gives it a *converso* slant. Through the correlation between a collective signifier ("nuestra vista") and a signified ("egibcio") that recalls the biblical suffering of the Jews, this semion metaphorically decrees that, like the Jews of the Old Testament, *conversos* must endure persecution in a land in which they had previously enjoyed better times.

Toward the end of the poem, after Amor rejects Viejo, he continues to torment the old man:

> Agora verás, don Viejo,
> conservar la fama casta;

aquí te veré do basta
tu saber y tu consejo.
Porque con sobervia y riña
me diste contradición,
seguirás estrecha liña[.] (Cota v. 523–29)

Two semions in these lines allude to the *converso* condition of Viejo. In one, the signifier "saber" is linked to the signified "sobervia," and in the other the signifier "consejo" is linked to the signified "riña." In being terms common to anti-Jewish discourse, "saber" and "consejo" evoke the Jewish lineage of Viejo. The persecution of the Spanish Jews was due in part to their mental superiority as perceived by Old Christians. In this light, Andrés Bernáldez declared that Jews were oppressed in Spain because their "herejía ovo su impinación e lozanía de muy gran riqueza y vanagloria de muchos *sabios e doctos,* e obispos, . . . e *sabios*" (in Castro, *Aspectos* 102). In his analysis of this passage, Castro notes:

> Dos veces usa Bernáldez la palabra *sabio* en el párrafo transcrito. Se perfilaba, en suma, en el horizonte una clase social con superioridad económica, científica, técnica y administrativa. . . . Se adormecía la Reconquista, nacía el comercio . . . reyes y señores empezaban a necesitar al pueblo no sólo para machucar terrones y pagar tributos; y al abrir los ojos a la nueva luz, resultaba que las más de las salidas estaban bloqueadas por aquellos circuncisos. (*Aspectos* 102)

> [Bernáldez twice uses the word "learned [man]" in the transcribed paragraph. In sum, a new social class with economic, scientific, technical, and administrative superiority was taking shape on the horizon. . . . The Reconquest was ending, commerce was beginning . . . kings and nobles were beginning to need the common people not only to plow the earth and pay tributes; and upon opening their eyes to this new order, it turned out that most of the (administrative) outlets were blocked by those who had been circumcised.]

Like the Jews, *conversos* frequently served the monarchy as royal advisors and in other capacities. Cota may even have occupied one of these posts himself; he is called a royal chronicler in the poem Montoro dedicated to him: "dizen que sois coronista / del señor Rey de Çeçilia" (Ciceri 173). Just as Jewish influence at court created friction between them and Christians, the success of *conversos* in royal service also inspired animosity among Old Christians, an attitude displayed in previously discussed poems by Juan de Dueñas and Suero de Ribera (see Chapter 1). During Cota's time, tensions between Old and New Christians were undoubtedly increased by the fact that the Catholic Monarchs, more than any prior regime, employed *conversos* in their retinues (Roth 117, 126–33).

The association of the signifiers "saber" and "consejo" to their respective signifieds produces a metaphor for the image of an inferior *converso*. Although they are by definition positive attributes, "saber" and "consejo" are undermined through their correspondence to "sobervia" and "riña," two terms with negative connotations. The inference here is that Viejo's "saber" and "consejo," because they are considered to be Jewish characteristics, will relegate him to a marginal existence, a notion evoked above by the phrase "seguirás estrecha liña." The term "estrecha" has a negative connotation: "Metafóricamente [estrecho] se suele usar por corto y de poca substancia, mísero, pobre y desdichado" (Cota 101, note 529).[13] The term "liña" was a shortened form of "línea" during the Middle Ages,[14] and was used to mean "path" in *cancionero* poetry (Cota 101, note 529). Sharing the social predicament visited on many *conversos*, Viejo is resigned to a harsh path, or destiny, because of the stigma attached to his intellectual capacities.

"Diálogo" reaches its climax when Amor and Viejo embrace. This occurs because Amor is able to convince Viejo that there will be a great reward if he accepts the opportunity to love again:

> De verdura muy gentil
> tu huerta renovaré,
> la casa fabricaré
> de obra rica, sotil.
> Sanaré las plantas secas
> quemadas por los friores;
> en muy gran simpleza pecas,
> viejo triste, si no truecas
> tus espinas por mis flores. (Cota v. 487–95)

In this passage, the micro-allegory and the historical backdrop of "Diálogo" are revealed. As I will demonstrate, the existence of this micro-allegory places theories that date the poem during the 1470s into question and suggests instead that "Diálogo" was composed during the late 1490s, after Cota's involvement with the Inquisition.[15]

On September 6, 1493, the Catholic Monarchs issued a decree directed toward the Jews who had converted during the previous years in order to avoid being expelled from Spain. In this decree, the Catholic Monarchs expressed their desire that these *conversos* become good converts by performing Christian acts and by assimilating into the Christian community:

> e por que nos deseamss [*sic*] que pues fuistes alunbrados por la gracia del Espíritu Santo vos saluéys e, dexadas las çerimonias e rritos de la ley vieja que ya dexastes en todo vos rrenovéys haziendo obras de católicos christianos . . . e tanvién escriuimos a los corregidores para que con vosotros tengan manera commo bivays entre católicos christianos e converséys con ellos por que de aquellos podáis ser enseñados e dotrinados syn que para ello por los vnos nin los otros se vos pongan penas pecuniales nin otras penas algunas. (Weill 60–61)

Cota's inclusion of the verb "renovaré" in Amor's pledge to rejuvenate Viejo ("tu huerta renovaré") allegorically alludes to the inefficaciousness of this royal plea for assimilation and religious harmony.[16] According to the decree, it was necessary for the *conversos* to act as good Christians in order to renew ("rrenovéys") their souls, the implication being that assimilation into the Old Christian community could be achieved by practicing Christianity. However, in calling for a unified Christian populace, the Catholic Monarchs completely disregarded the impediments that prevented *conversos* from assimilating, namely, the purity-of-blood statutes and the discriminatory practices of the Inquisition. By 1493 Cota had witnessed over forty years of persecution and would have been well aware that, contrary to the claims made by the monarchy, religious sincerity did not guarantee acceptance as a Christian.

The Catholic Monarchs' decree undoubtedly had a disheartening effect on Cota, who expresses his frustration with a semion in the final verse of the previously cited passage, in which the signifier "espinas" is linked to the signified "flores." The allusion produced by this correlation, to the promise of a brighter future if Viejo were to exchange his "espinas" for the "flores" offered by Amor (that is, if Viejo were to accept a renovated orchard), is subverted by Cota's own circumstances. When considered in this light, the ironic connotation of this correlation suggests that this semion is a reaction to the royal decree, which would situate the composition of "Diálogo" near the end of the fifteenth century. Another line in Amor's pledge may also have been inspired in Cota's personal situation. Amor's promise to rebuild Viejo's house ("la casa fabricaré") may have been incorporated into the micro-allegory in order to ironically recall the destruction of the Cota family home in 1449 and perhaps the confiscation of the poet's properties ("casas") by the Inquisition (as described in the previously mentioned document that refers to Cota as a "condenado").

As "Diálogo" continues, Amor recalls on the micro-allegorical level the cruelest punishment meted out by the Inquisition: "Este morava contigo / enel tiempo que me viste, / y por esto te encendiste" (Cota v. 208–10). The appearance in *converso* works of terms such as "encendiste" is thought to possess a particular significance. According to Cristina Arbós, "La idea de fuego va íntimamente ligada con la Inquisición en los Cancioneros" (the concept of fire is intimately connected to the Inquisition in songbooks) (82). A parallel example to "Diálogo" is found in the final two lines of a poem, "A la Reina doña Isabel," composed by Montoro during the mid-1470s. In the opening stanza he announces that his repeated attempts at integration have failed:

Hize el *Credo* y adorar
ollas de toçino grueso,
torreznos a medio asar,
oyr misas y rezar,
santiguar y persignar
y nunca pude matar
este rastro de confeso. (Ciceri 75)

In the last two lines, Montoro reiterates his resignation over the inevitable fate of the *conversos*. After making a plea to the queen, he employs a reference to "fuego" that demonstrates, in the words of Arbós, "un rasgo de humorismo amargo en el que parece mostrar su desconfianza en otra solución que no sea el fuego de la Inquisición" (a tone of bitter humor with which he seems to display his lack of faith in any solution other than the fire of the Inquisition) (82):

Pues Reyna de auctoridad,
esta muerte sin sosiego
çese ya por tu piedad
    y bondad
hasta allá por Navidad,
quando save bien el fuego. (Ciceri 76)

Another instance of the term "fuego" is found in the final lines of a previously discussed poem by Gómez Manrique (an Old Christian), "Coplas de Gómez Manrrique a Johan Poeta": "no por agua, mas por fuego / que anda cabo Sevilla" (*Cancionero castellano* 130). According to Márquez Villanueva, these lines evoke "the danger posed by the fledgling Holy Office" ("Jewish 'Fools'" 399, note 28).

Further on in "Diálogo," after they embrace, Amor asks Viejo what he feels: "Hete aquí bien abraçado: / dime, ¿qué sientes agora?" (Cota v. 514–15). The term "fuego" appears in Viejo's response, "Siento ravia matadora, / plazer lleno de cuydado; / siento fuego muy crescido" (Cota v. 516–18). In these lines, the term "fuego" forms part of a semion that alludes to Cota's involvement with the Inquisition. As such, "fuego" is a signified that is perceived by Viejo as "ravia matadora," a signifier that references a burning rage felt by a character representing Cota. The associative total may be understood as Cota's personal reaction to his indirect experience with the "fuego" of the Inquisition, that is, the burning at the stake in 1486 of Dr. Alonso Cota.

Finally, there is an interesting parallel between the name "Viejo" and Cota that further complements the micro-allegory. During his life the poet was referred to as Rodrigo Cota "a veces con el remoquete de 'el Viejo'" (at times with the sobriquet "the Elder") (Cantera Burgos, *El poeta* 21).[17] Cota may therefore have chosen to denominate his character "Viejo" in order to underscore the personal component of "Diálogo." As such, and at one and the same time, the character called Viejo symbolizes the *converso* caste in a macro-allegorical context while expressly signifying an autobiographical presence in the poem.

To review, the semions that inform Cota's poem are associations of terms and phrases that metaphorically allude to some of the major facets of anti-*converso* persecution:

Macro-allegory

Signifier	Signified
verduras, hollajes	linajes de natíos de eriales
ultrajes, desdenes	honor
nuestra vista	egibcio
saber	sobervia
consejo	riña

Micro-allegory

Signifier	Signified
espinas	flores
ravia matadora	fuego

As in the two other *converso* laments I consider in the following chapter, Diego de San Pedro's *Cárcel de amor* (1492) and Fernando de Rojas's

Celestina (1499), the oblique nature of Cota's semions speaks to the ominous presence of the Inquisition during its most active period. The recourse to allegory in *converso* laments distinguishes this mode of expression from previous works that were composed before the fate of the *conversos* had been sealed.

Cárcel de amor and Celestina as Converso Laments

While the *converso* allegory in *Cárcel* is not as complex as the two that inform Cota's poem, there are several points of contact between the works. To be sure, *Cárcel* does not appear to reflect of the personal experiences of San Pedro, who did not have a direct confrontation with the Holy Office. At the same time, during the course of establishing the inferiority of one protagonist in relation to another, both texts include semions that evoke the infliction of punishments by the Inquisition. In *Cárcel* this inferior condition is evident in the characterization of Leriano during his encounter with Persio and the king.

In San Pedro's book, Leriano is a noble gallant whose passion for Laureola, the daughter of King Gaulo of Macedonia, inspires him to travel to the Macedonian court in order to present his love suit to her. Once there, he is falsely accused of having a clandestine affair with Laureola and must confront his accuser, Persio, and eventually the king, in order to resolve the matter. Believing that his daughter is guilty, the king induces Persio to publicly challenge Leriano. Although Persio is defeated in combat, he continues to plot against Leriano; and the king, wrongly convinced that his own honor has been damaged, imprisons Laureola and condemns her to die. After several failed attempts to convince the king of Laureola's innocence, Leriano rescues her and Persio is killed. Even upon learning that Persio's accusations are untrue, the king prohibits Leriano from returning to the court until Persio's relatives have forgiven him. As the story draws to a close, Leriano dies of despair after Laureola refuses to see him.

I have underscored previously the importance of approaching *converso* texts with the idea that they are open to interpretation on multiple levels. Such is the case with *Cárcel*, which, like *Tractado de amores de Arnalte y Lucenda*, is informed by a surface narrative that focuses on the theme of courtly love. San Pedro's portrayal of Leriano as a courtly lover whose idealization of Laureola inspires him to become her amorous vassal typifies this theme. For Whinnom, it is Leriano's constancy, even in death, that enlists the gallant as the epitome of the "amante perfecto" (perfect lover):

> Todos los grandes amantes legendarios siguen intentando persuadirnos de que el amor perfecto debía ser eterno. . . . La *Cárcel de Amor* no se podía acabar de otra manera, no sólo porque San Pedro ha querido retratar al amante perfecto, sino porque para San Pedro el amor perfecto es necesariamente un amor constante. (San Pedro, *Obras II* 25)

> [All the great legendary lovers continue trying to persuade us that perfect love must be eternal . . . .*Cárcel de Amor* could not end in another manner, not only because San Pedro wants to portray the perfect lover, but because for San Pedro perfect love is necessarily a constant love.]

On one level of allegorical interpretation, Leriano may be understood as a representation of the exemplary courtly lover. In a contemporary social context, he may also represent a marginalized *converso*, whose thwarted attempt at achieving a physical union may allegorically allude to the arbitrary legal climate generated by the Inquisition.

As in *Tractado*, in *Cárcel* San Pedro invites the reader to discover a meaning concealed beneath the surface of his text: "Suplico a vuestra merced, antes que condene mi falta juzgue mi voluntad, porque reciba el pago no segund mi razón mas segund mi deseo" (*Obras II* 81). San Pedro's appeal to his patron, Diego Hernandes, might be read as a humble petition that his textual errors be excused. However, I submit that the distinction San Pedro makes between "razón" and "deseo" is the key to understanding this appeal in another sense. The term "razón," which, as Whinnom explains in his glossary to *Cárcel*, could mean "discurso, discusión, plática; dicho, palabras" (discourse, discussion, chat; remark, words) (San Pedro, *Obras II* 182), refers to the text itself. The term "deseo" refers to an intent behind the text, an inference reinforced by San Pedro's allusion, made a few lines before the appeal to his patron, to "otras cosas en lo que escrivo se pueden hallar" (*Obras II* 81). San Pedro tells his patron that he will receive his "pago," that is, comprehend the work, only if he takes this veiled meaning into account. It is interesting to speculate that San Pedro's preoccupation with the transmission of this meaning may relate to a concern that

Cárcel might be linked to *Tractado,* a possibility insinuated immediately before his reference to "otras cosas en lo que escrivo" (*Obras II* 81):

> Podré ser reprehendido si en lo que agora escrivo tornare a dezir algunas razones de las que en otras cosas he dicho. De lo cual suplico a vuestra merced me salve, porque como he hecho otra escritura de la calidad desta, no es de maravillar que la memoria desfallesca. (*Obras II* 80)

As Whinnom explains, "'otra escritura . . . desta': se refiere a *Arnalte y Lucenda*" ("'another work . . . [of the same quality as] this one': refers to *Arnalte y Lucenda*") (San Pedro, *Obras II* 80, note 10). Just as San Pedro's first sentimental novel possesses an underlying social theme announced in his dedicatory remarks, so too does *Cárcel.*

Both *Tractado* and *Cárcel* may be interpreted as *converso* texts that reflect their current sociohistorical environments. In *Tractado* the initial placement of San Pedro's laudatory poem to Queen Isabel establishes a foundation for a *converso* interpretation of *Tractado.* This foundation is created in *Cárcel* shortly after the story commences. In his opening words, the narrator, again called "auctor," reveals that the plot takes place "Después de hecha la guerra del año pasado" (San Pedro, *Obras II* 81). The reference to "la guerra" has been interpreted as an allusion to the campaign undertaken by the Catholic Monarchs in 1482 in order to defeat the Muslims of Granada (Whinnom in San Pedro, *Obras II* 25). *Cárcel* was therefore composed sometime between 1483, the year after that campaign began, and 1492, the year that the first known edition of the work was printed (Deyermond, *Diego de San Pedro* xli–xlii).

The action in *Cárcel* coincides with a period (1482–92) during which the Catholic Monarchs sought to end Muslim rule and solidify the Christian identity of early-modern Spain. The realization of their objective with the capture of Granada in 1492 was paralleled by a series of acts—the formal establishment of the Inquisition in 1480, the forced conversions of many remaining Jews and the expulsion of those who refused to convert in 1492, the same treatment of Spanish Muslims a decade later—that helped to forge Spain's "sociedad . . . ortodoxa" (orthodox society) (MacKay, *La España* 222). The Catholic Monarchs underscored this ideology in their Edict of Expulsion, in which the institutions of Church and nation are indistinguishable.[1] Although he could not have been responding to the Edict of Expulsion, which was issued after the first printing of *Cárcel,* San Pedro may have situated his story during the 1480s in order to suggest a parallel

between the political tone of *Cárcel* and the contemporary political climate. Specifically, the involvement of the monarchy in the marginalization of the *conversos* through its support of the Inquisition may have been
San Pedro's ideological backdrop. According to Márquez Villanueva, who
sees *Cárcel* as a reflection of this ideology,

> Diego de San Pedro no hace sino documentar . . . la existencia de un
> estado de ánimo muy lógico entre los conversos que acaban de
> presenciar y de sufrir las primeras actuaciones del Santo Oficio. . . . Su
> modo de reaccionar ante la Inquisición ha de entenderse en el campo
> en que él quiso formularlo, que es el de la crítica de una medida de
> gobierno. San Pedro la considera instrumento tiránico e hipócrita de
> una política anti-conversos. ("*Cárcel*" 196–98)

> [Diego de San Pedro does nothing less than document . . . the exist-
> ence of a very logical frame of mind among *conversos* who had just
> witnessed and endured the initial actions of the Holy Office. . . . His
> form of reacting to the Inquisition has to be understood in the context
> in which he wished to formulate it, that is, as a criticism of a form of
> government. San Pedro considers this (form of government) a hypo-
> critical and tyrannical instrument of an anti-*converso* policy.]

San Pedro's response to the recently established Inquisition is further defined by several semions in the text that depict Leriano's inferior status.
As *Cárcel* continues, auctor encounters Leriano in the Sierra Morena:

> vi salir a mi encuentro, por entre unos robredales do mi camino se
> hazía, un cavallero assí feroz de presencia como espantoso de vista
> . . . levava en la mano isquierda un escudo de azero muy fuerte, y en
> la derecha una imagen femenil entallada en una piedra muy clara, la
> cual era de tan estrema hermosura que me turbava la vista; salían
> della diversos rayos de fuego que levava encendido el cuerpo de un
> honbre quel cavallero forciblemente levava tra[s] sí. (San Pedro,
> *Obras II* 81)

Leriano's subsequent declaration, "En mi fe, se sufre todo" (San Pedro,
Obras II 81), contains a signifier, "fe," that hints at his *converso* identity.
Furthermore, evidence in the text suggests that this "fe" is part of an allusion to a particular moment in the trajectory of anti-*converso* persecution.
Leriano bemoans that, because of his faith, he is forced to endure great
suffering ("se sufre todo"), a condition that he exemplifies in being per-
petually tortured by "rayos de fuego" that "levava encendido [su] cuerpo"

(San Pedro, *Obras II* 81). The term "fe," which references Leriano's religious status, functions as a component of an allusion to the Inquisition by its association to "rayos de fuego," a phrase that contains a signified, "fuego," that characterizes Leriano's suffering in terms that recall anti-*converso* persecution by the Inquisition. As I discussed in the previous chapter, the appearance of the term "fuego" is thought to recall the punishment of burning at the stake. Because of their "fe"—that is, because they were inferior Christians—*conversos* were also made to suffer from "fuego," this signified serving to chronologically situate the metaphorical significance of Leriano's plight.

Other semions are found in the depiction of the aforementioned conflict between Leriano and Persio, an episode that for Márquez Villanueva (*"Cárcel"*) lies at the foundation of San Pedro's allegory. The conflict begins with Persio's false accusation that Leriano is having a clandestine affair with Laureola. Because much of the action that follows deals with the injustice done to Leriano as a result of this accusation, San Pedro underscores the slanderous nature of Persio's charges: "y no solamente dio fe a lo que veía, que no era nada, mas a lo que imaginava, que era el todo" (*Obras II* 113). From the outset, San Pedro reveals to the reader that Leriano is innocent and that Persio's discourse cannot be taken at face value.

Following Macedonian custom, Persio sends a letter to Leriano announcing the charge he has made. It begins with an explicitly ironic declaration. Although he has just been shown to be a liar, and unworthy of the trust placed in him by the king because of his supposed "virtud" (San Pedro, *Obras II* 114), Persio casts doubt upon Leriano's own virtue:

> Pues procede de las virtuosas obras la loable fama, justo es que la maldad se castigue porque la virtud se sostenga; y con tanta diligencia deve ser la bondad anparada, que los enemigos della si por voluntad no la obraren, por miedo la usen; digo esto, Leriano, porque la pena que recebirás de la culpa que cometiste, será castigo para que tú pagues y otros teman; que si a tales cosas se diese lugar, no sería menos favorecida la desvirtud en los malos que la nobleza en los buenos. . . . Pero venido eres a tiempo que recibieras por lo hecho fin en la vida y manzilla en la fama. (San Pedro, *Obras II* 114–15)

Márquez Villanueva considers these as "términos que, evidentemente, podrían ser aceptados por un inquisidor para cifrar lo más esencial de sus puntos de vista en materia religiosa" (terms that, evidently, could be accepted by an inquisitor in order to confirm his basic views on religious matters) inasmuch as they recall the "sentimientos odiosos que cuadran a un malsín y traidor" (hateful sentiments that are typical of an informer and a traitor) ("*Cárcel*" 194–95). If Persio's propensity for slander is used as a backdrop for interpreting the allusions he makes to Leriano's lineage, these allusions become semions that depict the inferiority of Leriano. According to Persio, Leriano's illicit relationship with Laureola constitutes an affront to his ancestral heritage:

> mal te has aprovechado de *la linpieza* [*sic*] *que heredaste.* ... Sin mirar ... *la obligación de tu sangre*, toviste osada desverguença para enamorarte de Laureola, con la cual en su cámara, después de acostado el rey, diversas vezes has hablado, escureciendo por seguir tu condición tu *claro linage*[.] (San Pedro, *Obras II* 114–15, emphasis added)

Persio then compounds his vilification of Leriano by declaring that he has come forward "tanto confiando en tu falsía y mi verdad" (San Pedro, *Obras II* 115). This remark couches his previous references to Leriano's genealogy in a disingenuous context.

These references form a semion with three signifieds (which could also be classified as three semions with the same signifier) that, at first glance, appears to allude metaphorically to the notion of an Old Christian bloodline. In each of these metaphorical associations, a signifier, Leriano, who is the subject of Persio's discourse, is linked to a signified, "limpieza que heredaste," "obligación de tu sangre," and "claro linage," which denotes Old Christian characteristics. Old Christians possessed inherited "limpieza" and a clear (or pure) "linage," and, because of his religious purity, an Old Christian would have been required to uphold the integrity ("obligación") of his "sangre" in matters of virtue. However, when considered in the context of the letter, the veracity of these associations is placed into question and it becomes clear that they are made in order to mock Leriano.

The fact that these semions appear at all in this letter reinforces this mockery. Persio composes his letter because he is obligated by local custom to present his charge in such a manner. The references to Leriano's lineage lie outside the bounds of his charge and are therefore out of place in his letter. Moreover, the fact that Leriano ignores these references in his epistolary response (San Pedro, *Obras II* 115–16) underscores the irony of their inclusion and encourages speculation regarding their significance. Just as Persio's accusation is a falsehood, so too is his description of Leriano's lineage. Leriano is not guilty of having an illicit relationship with Laureola just as he is not "guilty" of inheriting "limpieza" and a pure "linage," or of ignoring his "sangre." Rather than metaphorically alluding to Leriano in Old Christian terms, the semions impose upon him the same socioreligious inferiority that *conversos* were forced to endure and, in being false illusions, further suggest a parallel between Persio's charge and accusations that were launched against *conversos* without apparent reason.

Because of his lineage, Leriano is cast into an inferior position in the conflict that ensues. The king, believing that his daughter is guilty, induces Persio to challenge Leriano publicly. During the combat Persio loses his right hand, which leaves him defenseless and ready to accept his fate: "Haz lo que has de hazer, que aunque me falta el braço para defender no me fallece coraçón para morir" (San Pedro, *Obras II* 117). But rather than let justice take its course, which would rectify the situation inasmuch as Persio's accusation would be proven false, the king is persuaded (by Persio's relatives) to intervene and spare his life. This instance of random arbitration is incomprehensible to Leriano, who is unable to "pensar por qué el rey tal cosa mandase" (San Pedro, *Obras II* 118), and he seeks an explanation for the king's partiality:

> si por ventura lo consentiste por verte aquexado de la suplicación de sus parientes, cuando les otorgaste la merced devieras acordarte de los servicios que los míos te hizieron, pues sabes con cuánta costança de coraçón cuántos dellos en muchas batallas y conbates perdieron por tu servicio las vidas; nunca hueste juntaste que la tercia parte dellos no fuese. (San Pedro, *Obras II* 120)

In his commentary on this passage, Márquez Villanueva observes:

> Tan dura acusación de la ingratitud regia hacia los *suyos* sorprende por no responder a ninguna previa exigencia o necesidad funcional del argumento. Y la frase final está ahí para dejar bien en claro que el término *parientes* ha de entenderse en el sentido más lato. (*"Cárcel"* 194; Villanueva's emphasis)

> [Such a harsh accusation of royal ingratitude toward his *own* (relatives) is surprising in that it does not respond to any previous comment or essential component of the plot. And the final phrase is included in order to eliminate all doubt that the term *relatives* has to be understood in the broadest sense.]

Márquez Villanueva suggests that the king's decision to spare Persio's life, as well as Leriano's reaction, recalls the arbitrariness of the Inquisition

("*Cárcel*" 196). The presence of this social theme in *Cárcel* is further defined by a semion that underscores Leriano's inferior lineage. This semion is found after the narration of the combat between Leriano and Persio. San Pedro's reluctance to provide an extended description of the episode, which he calls a "cuento de historias viejas" (*Obras II* 117), indicates that he assumed that his public would be familiar with the nature of such events.[2] Such a familiarity would have naturally included the expectation "in accordance with ancient belief . . . [that] the will of God . . . [would] allow the victory of that party which was in the right" (*Poema de mio Cid* 138, note 3533). Indeed, the limited description that San Pedro does provide in *Cárcel* prepares the reader for such an outcome:

> sabiendo el rey que estavan concertados en la batalla, aseguró el canpo, y señalado el lugar donde hiziesen y ordenadas todas las cosas que en tal auto se requerían segund las ordenanças de Macedonia, puesto el rey en un cadahalso, vinieron los cavalleros cada uno aconpañado y favorecido como merecía; y guardadas en igualdad las honrras dentramos, entraron en el canpo; y como los fieles los dexaron solos, fuéronse el uno para el otro, donde en la fuerça de los golpes mostraron la virtud de los ánimos, y quebradas las lanças en los primeros encuentros, pusieron mano a las espadas. (*Obras II* 117)

However, this description of the confrontation contrasts with its result. Rather than justice, prejudice and haphazard legislation prevail. This injustice leads Leriano to launch his aforementioned plea: "si por ventura lo consentiste por verte aquexado de la suplicación de sus parientes . . . devieras acordarte de los servicios que los míos te hizieron" (San Pedro, *Obras II* 120). By creating a distinction between Persio's "parientes" and his own, Leriano evokes the concept of a discriminatory justice that randomly favors the lineage of Persio over his own bloodline.

Leriano's subsequent plea to the king is expressed in a manner that can be understood to reinforce the *converso* significance of the episode. Leriano asserts that he has the right to expect a just outcome of the dispute because, as the following quote implies, he is the social equal of Persio: "Si lo heziste por conpasión que havías de Persio, tan justo fuera que la huvieras de mi honrra como de su vida, siendo tu natural" (San Pedro, *Obras II* 120).[3] In spite of his claim that he is a social equal, and should therefore be afforded justice, Leriano is arbitrarily denied this opportunity, a situation that resembles the one faced by *conversos* who were randomly persecuted by the Inquisition.

In defining Leriano's inferiority, San Pedro employs a semion that participates in the discussion of honor initiated by Cartagena and Valera. The reference occurs in the king's response to a plea for Laureola's pardon made by the cardinal of Gausa. The king states that his decision was based on a conviction that his reputation would suffer if he were to display leniency:

> Si el yerro desta muger quedase sin pena, no sería menos culpante que Leriano en mi deshonrra. . . . y a tanto se estendería esta culpa si castigada no fuese, que podrié amanzillar la fama de los pasados y la honrra de los presentes y la sangre de los por venir; que sola una mácula en el linaje cunde toda la generación. (San Pedro, *Obras II* 132)[4]

According to the king, recognition of the relationship between Leriano and Laureola, which would be an indirect result of pardoning his daughter, would leave him and his entire family in "deshonrra." However, the king's inner conflict is irrelevant because his daughter does not need to be exonerated. Leriano's innocence had been all but proven on the field of combat, a resolution of the matter that the king neglected to take into account, as the cardinal of Gausa points out to him: "¿por qué das más fe a la información dellos que al juizio de Dios, el cual en las armas de Persio y Leriano se mostró claramente?" (San Pedro, *Obras II* 131).

By reminding the king of his partiality toward Persio, the cardinal of Gausa underscores the innocence of Leriano, and by extension the absence of an illicit relationship and the incongruity of the king's discussion of Laureola's punishment. The king's fear of "deshonrra" is dissociated from the alleged illicit relationship and linked to another source that represents a threat to his honor and lineage, a source that could only derive from Leriano's involvement in the matter (and possibly his intent to marry Laureola).[5] By extension, it is Leriano's lack of honor that causes the king to fear "deshonrra." Since Leriano has done nothing dishonorable, this must be an explicit comment on his dishonorable genealogy in relation to that of the king. The semion in the passage above that recalls this discriminatory attitude consists of the signifier "mácula," which references in intrusion of Leriano's bloodline, and the signified "deshonrra." The associative total of the correlation between "mácula" and "deshonrra," a metaphor that alludes to an individual whose lineage is inferior, inspires the notion that Leriano's lineage would indirectly be the cause of the king's "deshonrra" regardless of the existence of an illicit relationship. In other words, Leriano's lineage, like that of the *converso*, is the source of his inferiority.

Of course, by suggesting that Leriano is a representation of the marginalized *converso*, I am not denying that the semions that are used to depict him as such are open to multiple interpretations.[6] For example, Leriano's "fe" may also be understood as a reference to his devotion to Laureola. Similarly, the king's fear of "deshonrra" may also reflect the fact that an illicit relationship, if it existed, would be damaging to his honor in a paternal sense. As in Cota's poem, the semions in *Cárcel* reflect a tendency among *converso* laments to present such terms in a more oblique manner than works composed before the establishment of the Inquisition.

Unlike in the case of *Cárcel*, there is reason to speculate that Fernando de Rojas might have inscribed his own experiences into *Celestina*. If the evidence provided by Gilman is accurate (45), then Rojas may have been motivated to compose a *converso* lament similar in spirit to "Diálogo" after witnessing his father's execution by the Inquisition in 1488. However, Miguel Marciales has placed Gilman's findings into question, and subsequent attempts at instilling *Celestina* with an autobiographical presence have not satisfactorily resolved the issue of which elements in the text lend it a *converso* meaning. Several scholars have found this meaning in Rojas's supposed "Jewish" background. For example, in his commentary on Pleberio's lament after the death of Melibea (*Celestina* 336–43), Faur writes:

> It was next to impossible for anyone living in Puebla de Montalbán, Jew or *converso*, not to have been acquainted with Jewish values and ideas. In the case of Fernando de Rojas, he most probably had a solid Jewish education. He appears as an individual imbued with Jewish knowledge and sophistication. To the Sephardic reader the specific "Jewish" style of the character [Pleberio] is particularly striking: aphorizing, interlacing the speech with maxims and words of wisdom, and occasionally sparkling a sentence with rhyme prose. Sometimes the proverbs and maxims are so skillfully woven that they cannot be easily detected. This manner of speech characterized the educated Sephardi until modern times. (83–84)

In a related sense, Nepaulsingh considers Rojas to be one of "a few very clever [*converso*] writers [who] availed themselves of Maimonides' advice" (33) in the *Guide for the Perplexed* (which is a model for coded texts).[7] While these views are intriguing, and spring from a belief held by many critics (including myself) that Rojas veiled the *converso* meaning of *Celestina*, they superimpose an educational and cultural formation on Rojas that has yet to be corroborated by documentary evidence. In other words, they claim that *Celestina* reveals who Rojas was (or what he knew) rather than focusing on the text as a window into the social environment in which he lived and worked, which is one of the few aspects of his existence that cannot be disputed.

As Paul Julian Smith has observed, past attempts at reading *Celestina* as a *converso* text have not taken "the difference between author and character" (33) into account.[8] Although I do not deny that an autobiographical reading of *Celestina* might one day be possible if more information about Rojas becomes available, his personal experiences as a *converso* cannot currently be used as a point of departure for interpreting his work. At the same time, I do not concur with Smith that such a reading necessarily represses "the possibility that identity is provisional, writing intertextual, and meaning undecidable" (33). Interpretation depends on the perspective of the critic and allusions that acquire a particular significance when examined against a social backdrop may reveal different and unrelated meanings when examined in other contexts. This is the case with *Celestina*, which, like *Cárcel* and "Diálogo," allegorically alludes on one level of interpretation to the perils of worldy love and on another to the manner by which *conversos* were treated during the early decades of the Inquisition.[9]

As *converso* laments, *Cárcel* and "Diálogo" respond to the arbitrariness of accusations launched against *conversos* and the procedures of the Inquisition. Similarly, the *converso* allegory in *Celestina* derives from a set of semions that allude to the social climate forged by this arbitrariness, an "atmosphere of shared consternation and mutual suspicion" (44), in the words of Gilman. Rojas, like San Pedro, lays the foundation for this reading in the introductory sections of his work. The manner by which Rojas leaves passages in these sections open to multiple interpretations foreshadows the ambiguity with which he periodically depicts the genealogies of Calisto and Melibea.

In his introductory epistle, "El autor a un su amigo," Rojas infers that his text will be open to multiple interpretations. This facet of the book finds its roots in the manuscript that Rojas claims to have found and then incorporated as *auto* 1 of *Celestina* during "quinze días de unas vacaciones" (70).[10] Rojas reveals that he was compelled to read the manuscript on a number of occasions, and that different readings yielded different meanings:

Y como mirasse su primor, su sotil artificio, su fuerte y claro metal, su modo y manera de lavor, su estilo elegante, jamás en nuestra castellana lengua visto ni oýdo, leýlo tres o cuatro veces, y tantas quantas más lo leýa, tanta más necessidad me ponía de releerlo y tanto más me agradava, y en su processo nuevas sentencias sentía. (69–70)

In light of the admiration that he displays for the ingenuity of his model, it is not surprising that Rojas imitated its style by casting an ambiguous tone on his own text. In his acrostic poem ("El autor, escusándose de su yerro en esta obra que escrivió, contra sí arguye y compara"), Rojas incorporates the topos of *miscere utile dulci*, "Como el doliente que píldora amarga / o la rescela o no puede tragar, / métenla dentro del dulce manjar, / . . . / desta manera mi pluma se embarga" (73), in order to indicate that his text conceals a message designed to "atrae[r] los oýdos de penadas gentes" (73). Rojas's use of *miscere utile dulci* parallels other Spanish medieval works such as *El Conde Lucanor*, in which Juan Manuel employs the same topos in order to ensure that his readers "tomaren plazer de las cosas provechosas" (73). At the same time, while Manuel clearly appeals to the reader who seeks a more fulfilling existence ("E Dios . . . quiera que los que esto libro leyeren, que se aprovechen dél a servicio de Dios e para salvamiento de sus almas e aprovechamiento de sus cuerpos; así como Él sabe que yo, don Johan, lo digo a essa entención" [73]), the identity of "penadas gentes" is conspicuously ambiguous in *Celestina*.

In the final introductory section ("Prólogo"), Rojas provides a clue that may identify the "penadas gentes" who will hear *Celestina* being read: "Assí que quando diez personas se juntaren a oír esta comedia en quien quepa esta differencia de condiciones, como suele acaescer, ¿quién negará que aya contienda en cosa que de tantas maneras se entienda?" (80–81). Faur posits that Rojas's reference to a meeting of ten people ("quando diez personas se juntaren a oír") has a spiritual connotation: "A group of ten people has no special significance in Spanish; accordingly, it will pass unnoticed. For Jews, however, a group of ten people constitutes a *minyan*, or a minimum forum required for religious services and the reading of the Tora. For a *converso* 'a group of ten people' evokes the Jewish *minyan*. Indeed, Rojas seems to be alluding to a ritual reading. As with the public reading of the Tora, the ten people in the Prólogo do not read the text themselves, but are 'gathered to hear' ['se juntaren a oír'] it from a precentor" (72).

On one level of interpretation, the group of ten people attains a particular significance in a late fifteenth-century context. Given that *conversos* were frequently accused by the Inquisition of convening in order to pray in secret (which would have required a quorum, or *minyan*), the reference to "diez personas" might have been intended to signify that his work contained a message for those suspected of Judaizing. These *conversos* would consequently be the "penadas gentes." A closer reading of the context in which the allusion is placed, however, subverts the notion of a ritual reading of the Torah. According to Rojas those who unite will dispute the meaning of what they hear, precisely the opposite result of a reading of the Torah, which is realized in order to impart biblical doctrines. Moreover, in the preceding sentence Rojas casts doubt upon the probability that "diez personas" refers to a *minyan* by imposing a sense of irony upon the reference:

> Pero aquellos para cuyo verdadero plazer es todo, desechan el cuento de la hystoria para contar, coligen la suma para su provecho, ríen lo donoso, las sentencias y dichos de philósophos guardan en su memoria para trasponer en lugares convenibles a sus autos y propósitos. (80)

As Dorothy Severin explains in her note to this passage, "Debemos dudar de la sinceridad del consejo de Rojas si consideramos que la mayor parte de sus aforismos están puestos en boca de personajes corruptos y con propósitos cuando menos cuestionables" (We must doubt the sincerity of Rojas's advice if we consider that the majority of his aphorisms are placed in the mouths of corrupt characters that have questionable intentions) (Rojas 80–81, note 32). For the reader who grasps the irony in Rojas's introductory texts, the meaning of "diez personas" is again ambiguous.

This ironic tone, which, as María Rosa Lida de Malkiel (*La originalidad* 250–64) and Cándido Ayllón have illustrated, runs throughout the work, serves as the foundation for each of the semions in *Celestina*, semions composed of terms and phrases that appear to indicate the *converso* lineage of either Calisto or Melibea. However, they may be considered semions only when their superficial significance is subverted by the ironic contexts in which they occur. Thus these linguistic units serve as components of the allegorical meaning of *Celestina* by reproducing the atmosphere of suspicion created by the Inquisition. More specifically, the reader's inability to define the social identity of either protagonist parallels the type of conjectural accusations that often incriminated *conversos*.

The issue of whether Rojas's protagonists are representations of *conversos* has been a debated topic among scholars. Whereas Rodríguez Puértolas ("El linage") asserts that Calisto is the protagonist with a Jewish lineage, Fernando Garrido Pallardó, Orlando Martínez Miller, Emilio Orozco, and Segundo Serrano Poncela posit that Melibea is the *conversa*. These scholars have centered their arguments on a supposed impediment that prevents Calisto from marrying Melibea. Rodríguez Puértolas thus attributes the failure of their relationship to "la historia trágica, estremecedora, de una de tantas familias de origen judío caídas en la desgracia y el desdén sociales" (the tragic and startling story of one of many families of Jewish origin that had fallen into social disgrace and disdain) ("El linage" 216), while Orozco detects "las dificultades para unirse en matrimonio un caballero cristiano viejo con la hija de un poderoso judío converso" (the difficulties in uniting by marriage an Old Christian nobleman and the daughter of a powerful Jewish *converso*) (10). However, as Lida de Malkiel asserts, "[a]parte no haber nada en el texto que respalde tal hipótesis (lo mismo podría argüirse que es Calisto el converso y Melibea la cristiana vieja), cabe observar que el casamiento entre cristianos viejos y cristianos nuevos siempre fue lícito" ([a]side from there not being anything in the text that supports that hypothesis [the same argument could be made that Calisto is the *converso* and Melibea the Old Christian], it is worth noting that marriage between Old and New Christians was always legal) (*La originalidad* 208, note 8). Indeed, *conversos* had been marrying into Old Christian families for the greater part of the fifteenth century and continued to do so afterward without restrictions. Even if, as Netanyahu believes, there existed a contemporary fear among Old Christians "that Spain was on the eve of a flood of mixed marriages which would sweep away much of the nation" (*The Origins* 988), it is doubtful that a marriage fails to occur because of the social inferiority of either Calisto or Melibea.

Rojas's characterization of Calisto and Melibea excludes marriage as a possible option. As June Hall Martin has established, Calisto is a parody of the courtly lover. For Severin, the textual parallels between *Celestina* and *Cárcel* and the manner by which several components of Rojas's plot subvert that of San Pedro enlist Calisto as a parody of a particular courtly lover, Leriano, whom Severin deems the "quintaesencia del amante cortés" (quintessential courtly lover) (Rojas 29). Inasmuch as marriage is not an objective of courtly love, the fact that Calisto never mentions the subject has nothing to do with his lineage (or that of Melibea). In other words, Calisto never speaks of marriage because it would be uncharacteristic of him to do so. Marriage is certainly not an option for Melibea, as she expresses to her parents in *auto* 16: "no quiero marido, no quiero ensuziar los nudos del matrimonio, no las maritales pisadas de ajeno hombre repisar" (304). Although I concur with Martin and Severin in their assessments of Calisto, and believe that Melibea's declaration clearly indicates that Rojas did not intend to focus on the (im)possibility of a marriage, other references to Calisto and Melibea do suggest a *converso* presence in *Celestina*.

Just as Rojas may have reacted to his literary milieu by composing a parody of *Cárcel,* he may also have informed his text with a social dimension in order to react to his contemporary circumstances. At various junctures in the work Rojas includes semions that place the lineage of Calisto and Melibea in question through irony, suggesting that they might be *conversos.* To be sure, references to lineage frequently occur in *Celestina* in other contexts. For example, Pleberio's query, "¿Quién rehuyría nuestro parentesco en toda la cibdad?" (Rojas 302), and Alisa's reply, "que antes pienso que faltará ygual a nuestra hija, según virtud y tu noble sangre" (Rojas 303), spring from the desire of parents who are anxious to find a husband for their only daughter. On another occasion, Melibea's declaration, "no quiero ensuziar los nudos del matrimonio . . . como muchas . . . más discretas que yo, más subidas en estado y linaje" (Rojas 304–5), is meant to invoke the lofty status of women (Venus, Mira, and so on) who have broken the bond of matrimony. In the identification of the terms and phrases that I consider semions in the *converso* code, I treat only those references that are explicitly couched in contexts that may be interpreted on multiple levels, that is, the same type of interpretation that Rojas encourages in his introductory passages.

The first semion occurs in *auto* 2, during a dialogue between Calisto and his servant, Sempronio, who states: "Y dizen algunos que la nobleza es una alabança que proviene de los merescimientos y antigüedad de los padres. Yo digo que la agena luz nunca te hará claro si la propria no tienes. Y por tanto no te estimes en la claridad de tu padre, que tan magnífico fue, sino en la tuya" (131). Rodríguez Puértolas ("El linaje" 214) considers Sempronio's declaration that Calisto's father was "magnífico" as one of several instances in which Calisto's *converso* condition is recalled by its concealment. In other words, Calisto's father is called "magnífico" rather than "claro" (a term that should be understood to refer to pure lineage) because "magnífico" conceals Calisto's *converso* ancestry. However, the two terms are not mutually exclusive: the fact than an individual is called "magnífico" does not rule out the possibility that this person might be "claro" as well.

I submit that Sempronio's discourse contains a semion that suggests Calisto's *converso* lineage in a different manner. According to Sempronio's sources, nobility derives in part from the "antigüedad de los padres." By extension, this "antigüedad" may be considered a component of the "agena luz" that Calisto does not possess by birth (which is implied in the phrase "si la propria no tienes"). In other words, if Calisto had "antigüedad de los padres" he would be "claro," that is, pure (read pure Christian). Conversely, since he is not "claro," Calisto appears to be a representation of a *converso*. The semion in question therefore consists of an implied signifier that references Calisto's ancestry and the signified "claro." The correlation between these terms would appear to produce a metaphor for an Old Christian. However, this metaphor is subverted when considered in light of its alleged incongruousness as applied to Calisto, who does not possess the necessary "antigüedad de los padres" to be "claro." In this sense, the ironic inference of the semion is that he actually represents a *converso*.

It must be noted that I am not attempting to suggest that Sempronio represents here an Old Christian who scorns Calisto for his impure lineage; Sempronio underscores the importance of "antigüedad de los padres" because others have established this qualification (he begins by saying "Y dizen algunos"). This semion, as with other semions in *Celestina*, is more a comment on contemporary society rather than an explicit indication that the characters involved are representations of particular individuals in that society.

By including Sempronio's statement Rojas may also have wished to perpetuate a humanistic attitude embraced by earlier *converso* writers. In spite of the fact that *conversos* married into noble families, the act of questioning and affirming the nature of nobility had a particular meaning among *conversos* since the time of Cartagena, Valera, and Carrillo's circle. Calisto, as a representation of a *converso*, appears only to be worthy of virtue, and not nobility, because he does not possess the necessary lineage ("agena luz"). The best that Calisto can do is to attempt to be virtuous, as Sempronio explains: "De lo qual no el malo, mas el bueno, como tú, es digno que tenga perfecta virtud" (Rojas 131). However, Sempronio's following asseveration qualifies his previous comment by retaining an ideology held by previous *conversos* writers: "Y aun [más] te digo que la virtud perfecta no pone que sea hecho con digno honor" (Rojas 131). The humanistic attitude that Rojas perpetuates in these words is that, regardless of lineage, Calisto should, if he is virtuous, be able to acquire honor and, by extension, nobility.

The second semion that hints at Calisto's inferior lineage is found in *auto* 4. During their initial encounter, Celestina attempts to seduce Melibea by calling attention to Calisto's renown: "Bien ternás, señora, noticia en esta cibdad de un cavallero mancebo, gentilhombre de clara sangre, que llaman Calisto" (Rojas 161). Immediately after Celestina calls Calisto a "gentilhombre de clara sangre" Melibea reacts incredulously:

> ¡Ya, ya, ya, buena vieja, no me digas más! No pases adelante. . . . Si me hallaras sin sospecha desse loco, con qué palabras me entravas. No se dize en vano que el más empecible miembro del mal hombre o muger es la lengua. Quemada seas, alcahueta falsa, hechizera, enemiga de honestidad, causadora de secretos yerros. (Rojas 161)

Melibea's retort to Celestina provides the irony that casts doubt upon Calisto's alleged "clara sangre." The semion in question is formed by the correlation between signifier "gentilhombre," which references Calisto, and the signified "clara sangre," which recalls the notion of pure, or Old Christian, lineage. The associative total produced by this correlation appears to refer metaphorically to Calisto as an Old Christian. However, this image is contradicted by the tone of Melibea's retort. The sincerity of Celestina's remarks is placed into question by Melibea, as is the metaphor that is initially produced, which insinuates that Calisto might be a *converso* (if his "sangre" were not "clara").

Celestina's declaration that Calisto possesses "clara sangre" is one of two references to his lineage made by Celestina during her first meeting with Melibea. The second allusion made by Celestina, "De noble sangre, como sabes; gran justador" (Rojas 167), fails to produce a reaction, and Melibea shifts the focus of the conversation to the duration of his toothache: "¿Y qué tanto tiempo ha?" (Rojas 167). The difference between Melibea's reactions is significant, I believe, and reinforces the irony of the initial reference to Calisto's "clara sangre." Celestina follows the second reference with an indication ("como sabes") that the news of Calisto's nobility is, in fact, no news at all. The initial reference, however, is preceded by the phrase "Bien ternás" (Rojas 161), a grammatical construction that indicates that the speaker (Celestina) is not certain that the "noticia" (of Calisto's "clara sangre") is known by the listener (Melibea). Melibea is not incredulous upon hearing that Calisto is of "noble sangre" because she is already aware that he is noble. She is, however, surprised to hear Celestina's claim that he has "clara sangre" and labels this allusion a lie. The contrast between the two reactions enhances the parallel between Calisto and the *converso*. Although Calisto might pertain to a noble family, like the *converso* who achieved such nobility through kinship, he is unable to possess the lineage associated with true nobility in Old Christian society.

In *auto* 12, a declaration made by Calisto to Melibea introduces another semion that questions his ancestry: "O mi señora y mi bien todo, ¿por qué llamas yerro a aquello que por los santos de Dios me fue concedido? Rezando hoy ante el altar de la Madalena me vino con tu mensaje alegre aquella solícita mujer" (Rojas 263). This comment is overheard by Sempronio and Pármeno, and the latter responds by making a reference to Calisto's lack of religious conviction: "¡Desvariar, Calisto, desvariar! Por fe tengo, hermano, que no es cristiano" (Rojas 263). Calisto, the signifier as the subject of "es," is linked to a signified, "no cristiano," in response to his declaration that he has performed a Christian act (praying at "el altar de la Madalena"). The allusion produced is to a Christian individual who is not really Christian even though he behaves like one, that is, an inferior *converso*. In addition, Calisto's decision to practice his religious beliefs at the "altar de la Madalena" also points toward his *converso* identity inasmuch as Mary Magdalene is herself a convert (from prostitution to the doctrines of Jesus [Luke 7.37–50]).

Of course, this semion may be understood in a different sense when considered from another perspective. Calisto's declaration that his relationship to Melibea has been divinely sanctioned, "¿por qué llamas yerro a aquello que por los santos de Dios me fue concedido?" (Rojas 263), certainly forms part of Rojas's parody of the courtly lover. On other occasions Calisto is also characterized as a suspect Christian for his exaggerated descriptions of his love for Melibea. In *auto* 1 Sempronio calls him a "herege" (Rojas 92), questions his religious affiliation ("¿Tú no eres christiano?" [Rojas 93]), and inquires ("¿Y assí lo crees, o burlas?") if Calisto is serious when he calls Melibea a "¡Dios, Dios!" (Rojas 95). At the same time, the semion in *auto* 12 is placed in a particular context that invites the critical scrutiny that Rojas encourages.

The final semion dealing with Calisto is located in *auto* 20. Moments before she commits suicide, Melibea informs her father, "Conosciste assimismo sus padres y claro linage; sus virtudes y bondad a todos eran manifiestas" (Rojas 333). The semion is formed by the correlation between

Calisto, the signifier as the implied subject of Melibea's remark, and the signified "claro linage," which denotes pure lineage. Once again, the associative total denotes an individual of pure lineage, which suggests that Calisto metaphorically represents an Old Christian. However, this allusion to Calisto cannot be taken at face value. Melibea's apparent reference to the purity of Calisto's lineage ("claro linage") is contradicted by her allusion to his "virtudes and bondad," two attributes that Calisto does not display in *Celestina*. Inasmuch as the insincerity of Calisto's actions and words masks a character that has been classified as egocentric (Lida de Malkiel, *La originalidad* 347), greedy, lustful, and corrupt (Martin 113, 126), and "places him morally on the level of the servants and prostitutes" (Martin 126), Melibea's assessment of his lineage must be understood in an ironic context. Just as he is not virtuous or kind, in contrast to what Melibea claims, Calisto does not demonstrate that he is of pure lineage. In fact, there is no indication in *Celestina* that Pleberio has ever met Calisto's parents (who never appear in the work), as Melibea also claims ("Conosciste assimismo sus padres"), which further undermines the veracity of the metaphor produced by the semion.

Irony also informs two semions that suggest that Melibea is a *conversa*. In *auto* 1, Calisto declares, "Sempronio, sin proporción ni comparación se aventaja Melibea. Miras la nobleza y antigüedad de su linaje, el grandísimo patrimonio, el excelentíssimo ingenio, las resplandecientes virtudes, la altitud y ineffable gracia, la soberana hermosura" (Rojas 100). The semion here is formed by the correlation between "Melibea," the signifier as the subject of Calisto's discourse, and "nobleza y antigüedad de su linaje," a signified that denotes a pure ancestry. By calling attention to the "nobleza y antigüedad" of Melibea's "linaje," Calisto appears to be creating a metaphor for an Old Christian individual. However, this remark is discredited, and Melibea's lineage brought into question, when it is considered for its ironic inclusion among the other attributes mentioned by Calisto, all of which are confirmed on other occasions in the text. Melibea's patrimony ("grandísmo patrimonio") is demonstrated by the wealth that her family obviously possesses. Although she eventually commits the unchaste act of having intimate relations with Calisto, Melibea has preserved her virtue ("resplandecientes virtudes") to this point by rejecting Calisto in the dialogue that opens the work. She displays her "excelentíssimo ingenio" (and, by her own declaration, her "virtud") in this rejection by outwitting Calisto, that is, by making him believe for a moment that his attempt to seduce her will be successful and then by mocking him and turning his hope of receiving a "galardón" into despair:

Calisto: Téngolo por tanto, en verdad, que si Dios me diesse en el cielo la silla sobre sus santos, no lo ternía por tanta felicidad.

Melibea: Pues, ¡aún más ygual galardón te daré yo, si perseveras!

Calisto: ¡O bienaventuradas orejas mías que indignamente tan gran palabra avéys oýdo!

Melibea: Más desventuradas de que me acabes de oýr, porque la paga será tan fiera qual [la] meresce tu loco atrevimiento, y el intento de tus palabras [Calisto] ha seýdo *como* de ingenio de tal hombre como tú aver de salir para se perder en la virtud de tal mujer como yo. ¡Vete . . . torpe! que no puede mi paciencia tolerar que haya subido en coraçón humano conmigo el ilícito amor comunicar su deleyte. (Rojas 87)

Finally, Melibea's "gracia" and "hermosura" are attested by Calisto's extended description of her (Rojas 100–101) that follows his aforementioned reference to her "soberana hermosura."

The "nobleza y antigüedad" of Melibea's lineage cannot therefore be said to allude to the purity of her lineage, as the semion suggested. On the contrary, among the attributes Calisto attributes to Melibea these are the only two that appear to be contradicted by the text: Pleberio, her father, is a merchant and there is no indication that he possesses a noble title. The fact that these attributes are contradicted by the text subverts the notion of Melibea's "nobleza y antigüedad de . . . linaje" and provides grounds for speculating that she is actually a *conversa*.

In *auto* 12, Melibea's possible *converso* status is again evoked by a comment made by Calisto: "Pero como soy cierto de tu limpieza de sangre y hechos, me estoy remirando si soy yo Calisto a quien tanto bien se [le] haze" (Rojas 261). The semion in this passage is created by the correlation between the signifier "Melibea," who is the subject of Calisto's comment, and "limpieza de sangre," a signified that is once again synonymous with pure lineage. As in the cases of other semions in *Celestina*, the associative total is a metaphor that appears to allude to an Old Christian. However, the irony of Calisto's conviction is revealed when "limpieza de sangre" is considered in light of his claim that Melibea's "hechos" also demonstrate "limpieza," which subverts his conviction since she has just committed the "impure" act of surrendering herself to Calisto. In other words, just as her "hechos" are impure so too is her "sangre." The metaphorical value of this last association is again contradicted and doubt is therefore cast on Melibea's alleged "limpieza de sangre."

The terms that Melibea uses upon yielding to Calisto, "Todo lo que te dixo confirmo; todo he por bueno; limpia, señor, tus ojos; ordena de mí a tu voluntad" (Rojas 261), enhance the possibility that she does not possess "limpieza de sangre." Melibea's request that Calisto "limpia ... [sus] ojos" recalls a stanza from Rojas's introductory acrostic poem:

Limpiad ya los ojos, los ciegos errados,
virtudes sembrando con casto bivir,
a todo correr devéys de huyr,
no os lance Cúpido sus tiros dorados. (Rojas 75–76)

Contrary to the "ciegos errados," who are told to dry their eyes (a metaphor for ridding themselves of carnal sins) in order to dissociate themselves from physical love, Melibea's request that Calisto perform the same act evokes the future consummation of their relationship. In Melibea's request, the term "limpia" is thus a metaphor for impurity; likewise, her "hechos," and by extension her "linage," are not what Calisto claims them to be, suggesting that she is actually a *conversa*.

By using semions that question the ancestries of Calisto and Melibea, Rojas inscribes *Celestina* with a *converso* allegory that responds to the social atmosphere of the late 1490s. As in *Cárcel*, this allegory is revealed through irony. To review, the allegory in *Cárcel* is a political reaction, whose presence is suggested by San Pedro before the plot commences, to the establishment of a legal system that discriminated against *conversos*. The associations between signifiers and signifieds reflect the tension of the historical moment and perturbation over the inferior condition imposed on *conversos* by the intensity and randomness of scrutiny by the Inquisition:

Semions in *Cárcel de amor*

Signifier	Signified
fe	fuego

Explanation of semion:
The association of these terms is chronologically situated between 1483 and 1492 by the mention of "la guerra del año pasado." A parallel is therefore suggested be-

tween certain events depicted in *Cárcel* and the type of discrimination practiced
by the recently established Inquisition.

Signifier	Signified
Leriano (the implied subject)	1. limpieza que heredaste
	2. obligación de tu sangre
	3. claro linage

Explanation of semion:
Associations of terms that accuse Leriano of possessing a socioreligious inferiority
as understood against the backdrop of Persio's disingenuous discourse. Since these
accusations are launched without apparent cause, they recall the practice of making false accusations against *conversos*.

Signifier	Signified
mácula (in reference	deshonrra
to Leriano's lineage)	

Explanation of semion:
This association is intended to suggest Leriano's "guilt" in a genealogical sense by
asserting that his lineage, rather than his involvement in an alleged illicit relationship, is the reason for his inferiority.

The semions in *Celestina*, some of which are composed of associations
of terms similar to those in *Cárcel*, suggest New Christian ancestries for
both Calisto and Melibea. One might conclude that the fact that most of
these inferences are made by persons of dubious character, including
Sempronio, Celestina, Pármeno, and Calisto, is meant to recall "testimony
[before the Inquisition] from witnesses who would not ordinarily be accepted because of disqualifying characteristics, including those considered
infamous" (Peters 92). In other words, Rojas re-creates his contemporary
environment, the aforementioned "atmosphere of shared consternation
and mutual suspicion" (44) described by Gilman, by casting suspicion on
the characters who cast suspicion on others through their remarks. Rojas
invests his work with discourse that imitates the contemporary terms by
which *conversos* were accused of heresy. It is interesting to speculate
whether his depictions of the accusers provide a personal testimony of the
consternation felt by one particular *converso* over the existence of a legal
system that accepted evidence given by suspect individuals.

Semions in *Celestina* that place Calisto's lineage in question

Signifier	Signified
Calisto's ancestry	claro
(an implied signifier)	

Explanation of semion:
In associating these terms, Sempronio questions Calisto's social status inasmuch as Calisto does not possess the "antigüedad" necessary to be *claro*, and thus implies that he represents a *converso*.

Signifier	Signified
gentilhombre	clara sangre

Explanation of semion:
Celestina apparently associates these terms in order to underscore Calisto's pure ancestry. Melibea's subversion of this association suggests that his "sangre" is not "clara," or pure Christian.

Signifier	Signified
es (referring to Calisto)	no . . . cristiano

Explanation of semion:
Calisto is called a "no cristiano" by Pármeno in spite of his performance of a Christian act (praying at the altar of the Magdalene), the inference being that, like the *converso*, his religious sincerity does not afford him equal standing as a Christian.

Signifier	Signified
Calisto (the implied subject)	claro linage

Explanation of semion:
The association between these terms is subverted by Melibea's subsequent reference to Calisto's "virtudes" and "bondad." Since he is neither virtuous nor kind, Calisto's lineage is not "claro."

Semions in *Celestina* that place Melibea's lineage in question

Signifier	Signified
Melibea (the implied subject)	nobleza y antigüedad de su linaje

Explanation of semion:
The contradiction of this association by the lack of evidence to establish the nobility of Pleberio casts a shadow on Melibea's purported Old Christian attributes and suggests that she actually represents a New Christian.

Signifier	Signified
Melibea (the implied subject)	limpieza de sangre

Explanation of semion:
These terms are associated by Calisto concurrent to his declaration that Melibea's "hechos" also illustrate "limpieza," an inaccurate evaluation of her actions that undermines his assessment of her "sangre" and implies that she is a *conversa*.

These semions reproduce the experience of living as a potentially suspect Christian. Moreover, Rojas's characters exist in a universe shaped by the ominous threat that the Holy Office could represent. The consternation created by the practices of that institution resonates in Celestina's revelation that Pármeno's mother was forced to make a false confession: "Mira si es mucho passar algo en este mundo por gozar de la gloria del otro, y más que según todos dezían, a tuerto y [a] sinrazón y con falsos testigos y rezios tormentos la hizieron aquella vez confessar lo que no era" (Rojas 199). The same attitude is reflected in the apparent haphazardness with which Rojas placed his semions in the text. Due to the ambiguity of the references, and the fact that they are made for the most part by characters whose discourse inspires little confidence, the reader of *Celestina* is unable to determine clearly who Calisto and Melibea really are. The fact that the reader cannot be sure of a character's socioreligious identity may be understood as another reflection by Rojas on his contemporary social reality. In being presented with uncertain information, the reader is afforded a glimpse into the psychology of living with a lineage that could subject an individual to charges of heretical acts made by less than credible accusers.

The doubt that surrounds the identities of Calisto and Melibea is the essence of Rojas's *converso* allegory. When the two become victims of "fortune's mutations" (Gilman 176), the reason for their adversity is as nebulous as their socioreligious conditions. Why are Calisto and Melibea destined to live and die (without making confessions) outside the bounds of contemporary society? It may be because Rojas is condemning the type of illicit affair in which they engage, or it may be because one or both characters represent a figure that has been relegated to a marginal existence. The fact that the reader is unsure about Calisto and Melibea does not necessarily make them *conversos*. But it does make them suspect individuals, and this, if nothing else, reflects the contemporary mistrust among individuals that could result in persecution by the Inquisition, perhaps through an accusation brought by a friend or by one family member against another. In being a *converso* lament, *Celestina*, like *Cárcel* and "Diálogo," reveals how *conversos* could be treated during the last decades of the fifteenth century.

8

Toward an Evaluation
of the *Converso* Code

In this book I hope to have bridged a significant gap in the field of *converso* studies, namely, the relationship between the history of the *conversos* and their literature. General historical assessments recognize that *conversos* were considered to be inferior Christians because they were treated as Jews. As Paul Johnson has stated concisely in one of the most recent studies of the period, "A Spanish Jew found he could not evade anti-Semitic hostility by converting" (224). Yet some scholars who discuss contemporary literature continue to deny that this historical reality influenced the literature of the *conversos*. In the words of Roth, "Many Hispanists, indeed, have claimed to detect a 'converso mentality' in the literature [of the fifteenth through seventeenth centuries]. Lacking any precise definition, this term seems to smack at least of romanticism, if not worse, and is largely nonsense. It would seem that whatever is found reflected in Spanish literature of the period is simply labeled 'converso mentality.' What would be required is a detailed analysis, so far not attempted, of the writers and their work as a whole group, with a view to determining what, if any, Jewish or 'converso' influences may have been at work" (158). In this book, I have attempted to fill the lacuna pointed out by Roth. By situating *converso* works in their sociohistorical contexts, I have aspired to demonstrate that an understanding of *converso* literature derives from comprehending the divergences among *converso* experiences.

A review of the stages by which the *converso* code evolved reinforces this point. While the semions in each of these stages reveal the inferiority of the *conversos*, they do so from unique perspectives. The corpus of works involving Juan Poeta demonstrates that the presence of semions in Old Christian works does not necessarily indicate animosity on the part of the author toward *conversos*. Likewise, the semions in works by Poeta are not necessarily assertions of his sincerity as a Christian. At the same time, the existence of these semions in a variety of Old Christian and *converso* works composed after 1449 indicates an awareness of the nature of the social decline of the *conversos* after the Toledo rebellion. The terms and phrases involved explicitly associate a Christian with a Jew, which was the basis for discrimination against *conversos* in the Sentencia-Estatuto and subsequent purity-of-blood statutes.

The advent of anti-*converso* discrimination inspired the first stage in the *converso* code. Taking their cue from the foundation laid by Cartagena and Valera, the writers of Carrillo's circle disseminated humanistic ideas that advocated equality between New and Old Christians. The legacy of this early humanism, exemplified by semions in works by Álvarez Gato and Guillén, ironically left an enduring imprint on the character of Spanish Renaissance ideology. These authors, and other *conversos* who did not employ semions, expressed humanistic ideals in the name of a reformed Christianity, so as to promote their ideological acceptance as Christians. However, in the long run, the acceptance of this reform within Spain was to come at the expense of a unified Christian populace. While the Inquisition intensified its effort to exclude those who were considered to be inferior Christians, the course of humanism in Spain during the Renaissance continued to define itself in terms of a return to the orthodox doctrines of the Christian faith (as opposed to the tendency toward a relaxation of Christian dogma that defined the movement in other parts of Europe).

It is also interesting to consider the possible influence of *converso* writers on the spread of humanism throughout Castile. Scholars such as Round (204) argue that humanism took longer to gain a foothold among the Castilian nobility than among its European counterparts. If this is true, then perhaps the reason for what Round terms a "dishonourable" association between the nobility and the "pursuit of learning" (206) was a reluctance by influential Old Christian noblemen to embrace the egalitarian character of early humanism. Another possible explanation is that these noblemen wished to distance themselves from *converso* humanists, whose intellectual activities may have been associated with their inherent lack of honor.

The following stage of the *converso* code attempted to alter the political destiny of the *conversos*. The nationalization of anti-*converso* persecution during the 1460s inspired several *conversos* to attack King Enrique IV for his collusion in this social phenomenon. While Enrique's policies helped to ensure that pogroms and purity-of-blood statutes became regular and unchecked occurrences, the creation of a Spanish Inquisition, although supported by the king, was not yet an inevitability due to his lack of political authority. The semions employed by *conversos* who deified Queen Isabel reflect their hope that the recently crowned queen would reverse their social decline, and the terms that compose these semions demonstrate that *conversos* writing during the mid-1470s were aware of the collective nature of their plight. Although it had not yet been fully implemented, Espina's plan to deal with the *conversos* gave an aggregate voice to popular sentiment, which deemed *conversos* inferior Christians because their ancestors had been Jewish. Whereas semions in the initial stage of the *converso* code reflect a faith in the capacity of humanistic reforms to redefine the relationship between New and Old Christians, the optimism that informs the semions in poems dedicated to Isabel is tempered by a realization that the reformist movement had failed. This modified outlook is evident in the difference between the signifiers that reference the *conversos*. In poems that espouse humanistic ideals, collective signifiers, "somos" and "todos," are used in order to suggest that *conversos* might be included as members of a united Christian community. In contrast, poems dedicated to Isabel include semions with collective signifiers, "nuestro," "nuestra," and "nuestras," that participate in allusions to the victimization of the *converso* community, indicating that social treatment of the *conversos* as the Other was now felt to be a shared experience.

Ultimately, the Catholic Monarchs did not bring together a nation that lived up to the ideals of *converso* writers who sought to integrate into Spanish Christian society. Instead, the establishment of the Inquisition meant that *conversos*, regardless of their actions, would continue to be deemed inferior because of their Jewish heritage. The next stage in the *converso* code, the *converso* lament of the late fifteenth century, communicates the fear of revealing one's *converso* identity after decades of exposure to fortune's mutability. This adversity is evident in each work's depiction of the decline of its protagonists, which recalls the perils of the early decades of the Inquisition. At the same time, each *converso* lament provides a unique perspective on this theme. San Pedro's *Cárcel* represents an early reaction to the imposition of an arbitrary and discriminatory legal system, Cota's "Diálogo" speaks to the hypocrisy of the monarchy that supported the Inquisition, and Rojas's *Celestina* is ruled by the treachery by which that institution operated during its most active period.

Each of these works is also an allegory that veils its social meaning to a different extent. I would argue that the obliqueness with which these meanings are concealed becomes increasingly pronounced as the last two decades of the fifteenth century evolved. The most elaborate episode in *Cárcel* is the dispute between Leriano and Persio (including the king's arbitrary decision), and this is precisely the episode that suggests a *converso* reaction to the recent establishment of the Inquisition by the monarchy. The *converso* meaning in "Diálogo" is more obscure. Without explicitly recalling any of the persecutors of the *conversos*, Cota paints a general portrait of the contemporary socioreligious climate by alluding to facets of the inferior status of New Christians. In *Celestina* the interpreter is forced to speculate with greater uncertainty in order to make conjectures concerning the socioreligious identities of the protagonists. The reader of the pages that I have dedicated to *Celestina* might wonder why I have not included a discussion of the lament made by Pleberio after Melibea's death. The reason is simple: I have not found enough evidence to identify any semions in this passage. However, given the ambiguity of the semions I have identified, and the fact that these associations must be subverted in order to discover their *converso* meanings, I am confident that Rojas would not have included such discourse in what many consider the most significant monologue in the work. Those scholars who have seen explicit references in Pleberio's lament to *converso* themes or to Rojas's personal situation have not, I believe, captured the spirit of Rojas's allegory. As I suggested in Chapter 7, Rojas's apparently random placement of his semions forms a component of his allegory. Different characters make the correlations between terms and phrases, the semions occur in a variety of contexts, and the metaphors they produce cast doubt on the lineages of both protagonists. By crafting his allegory in this fashion, Rojas reproduces his own social environment.

My study has shown that the *converso* meaning of the texts under consideration is best defined from the sociohistorical perspectives of those who were considered as Others. As I have demonstrated, the *converso* code is not one literary voice but an aggregation of voices. At the same time, these voices were inspired by similar (albeit changing) circumstances to employ literature as a vehicle for expressing socially motivated themes. Although the themes that surface are not restricted to *converso* texts, their incorporation by *converso* authors is tied to the evolution of the social rift between Old and New Christians. While Old Christian writers also embraced humanism, *conversos* were motivated to participate in the movement because humanistic ideals supported their equality as Christians at a time when that equality was initially being denied. Old and New Christians received the ascension to the throne of Queen Isabel with enthusiasm, but the fact that *conversos* consistently chose to deify her reflects their hope that her regime would produce social harmony. The theme of fortune's mutability was popular among a variety of medieval Spanish writers, but only the *converso* lament consistently expresses it during a period in which the *conversos* suffered the greatest adversities. Of course, *conversos* were certainly not the only victims of the Inquisition. However, the *converso* lament stands out as a particularly *converso* reaction to being the principal targets of that institution. As a mode of literary expression, the *converso* code of the late fifteenth century does not create *converso* history. The *converso* code is a collection of distinct literary voices that re-creates the diversity by which that history was forged.

Notes

Chapter 1. The *Conversos:* A Historical Overview

1. The name "Sephardim" derives from the term "Sepharad," which is employed in the book of Obadiah (v. 20) to refer to the place where the Jews of Jerusalem were exiled during the sixth century B.C.E.. It became the Hebrew name for Spain.

2. James Parkes (345–70) provides a good overview of the attitude of the Visigoths toward both Jews and Jewish converts to Christianity.

3. See Parkes (356–57) for more on the Fourth Council of Toledo.

4. For more on the contributions of Jews to Spanish economies between 1150 and 1230, see Yitzhak Baer (1:78–90).

5. Jews are associated with the devil in *cantigas* 3 and 9, involved in ritual killings in *cantigas* 4 and 6, and portrayed as greedy in *cantiga* 25.

6. For more on the attitude toward Jews in Las Siete Partidas, see Carpenter's study and notes in his thorough critical edition of the text, and for a discussion of the emblem Jews were required to wear, see Carpenter (99–101).

7. In addition to O'Callaghan and Carpenter, Castro also depicts Alfonso X as a monarch who desired to protect the Jews and include them in his society (*La realidad* 38–40, 44).

8. On the role of Jews at the court of Alfonso X, see Castro (*España* 454–64).

9. For a discussion of the contributions of Jews to the government of Alfonso X, see Baer (1:118–29).

10. See Baer (1:310) and Julio Valdeón Baruque ("Motivaciones socioeconómicas" 86, note 19).

11. For more on the relationship between the mendicant orders and Jews during the thirteenth century, see Jeremy Cohen.

12. On the attribution of outbreaks of the Black Plague to the Jews, see the discussion by Trachtenberg (102–6).

13. See Angus MacKay (*La España* 186–87).

14. For more on the role of Jews as tax collectors, see M. A. Ladero Quesada.

15. On the status of the Castilian Jews during the conflict, see Valdeón Baruque (*Los judíos*).

16. On the events of 1391, see Philippe Wolff, and MacKay, "Popular Movements and Pogroms in Fifteenth-Century Castile."

17. See Márquez Villanueva ("Conversos y cargos concejiles") for an examination of this rise in anti-*converso* sentiment.

18. See Vendrell de Millás for a critical edition of this poem.

19. See MacKay for a discussion of the inflationary crisis that occurred prior to 1449 ("Popular Movements" 53).

20. Juan II was unable to resolve the economic problems that had been plaguing Castile for centuries, and by the middle of the 1440s his kingdom was suffering through a period of renewed inflation and food shortages (MacKay, *Spain* 186).

21. See Eloy Benito Ruano (*Toledo* 191–96) for the complete text of the Sentencia-Estatuto.

22. For more on the purity-of-blood statutes, see Antonio Domínguez Ortiz (*Los judeoconversos en España y América* 79–104, *La clase social* 53–79); Kamen (*The Spanish Inquisition: A Historical Revision* 233–42); and Albert Sicroff.

23. See Fernán Pérez de Guzmán (674–75) for an account of the imposition of these penalties by Juan II.

24. See Benito Ruano (*Toledo* 74–76, 216–20, 222–23).

25. See Benito Ruano (*Toledo* 215–16, 223–27). In 1451 the pope did, however, affirm his condemnation of the Sentencia-Estatuto (Benito Ruano, *Los orígenes* 73).

26. In order to secure peace, in 1468 Enrique IV named his half sister, Isabel, as his successor.

27. MacKay posits a correlation between the deterioration of the economy and the escalation of anti-*converso* hostilities during Enrique IV's reign:

> From 1445 onwards . . . there was a high degree of price inflation which reached serious proportions by the 1460s and 1470s. At the same time, subsistence crises occurred more frequently and culminated in the widespread crisis of 1469–73 when the prices of grain and other foodstuffs, especially in Andalucía, reached catastrophic heights. These were the years of endemic urban unrest which led up to the pogroms of 1473.
>
> The economic background helps to explain why unrest was predominantly, but not exclusively, anti-semitic in nature. . . . As nominal prices rose so did the price of tax-farms, and this resulted in an obvious increase in taxes for which, of course, Jews and *conversos* were held responsible. (*Spain* 186)

28. The events of 1467 are described in Benito Ruano (*Toledo* 93–110).

29. For more on Espina and the *Fortalitium*, see Baer (2:283–92) and Netanyahu (*The Origins* 726–43).

30. See Netanyahu (*The Origins* 736–40) for more on this request.

31. Baer (2:289–92) describes some of the activities of this episcopal Inquisition, which was headed by the leader of the Jeronimite Order, Alfonso de Oropesa.

32. See Peggy Liss for more on Isabel's attitude toward the Jews.

Chapter 2. The Theoretical Parameters of the *Converso* Code

1. My definition of *concepto* parallels the one offered during the seventeenth century by Baltasar Gracián: "Consiste, pues, este artificio conceptuoso, en una primorosa concordancia, en una armónica correlación entre dos o tres cognoscibles extremos, expresada por un acto del entendimiento" (239).

2. For other types of *conceptismos* in *cancionero* poetry, see Keith Whinnom (*La poesía* 47–62).

Chapter 3. The Poetic Dialogues Involving Juan Poeta

1. Rodríguez Puértolas provides the most recent biography of Montoro in his introduction to Ciceri's critical edition of his poetry (Ciceri 11–30).

2. "Alfaquí," as Jauralde Pou explains, is a reference to the "sabio o sacerdote docio entre los árabes" (learned man or docile priest among the Arabs) (*Cancionero de obras* 88, note 26).

3. For more on Poeta's career as a customs official in Palermo, a post that some scholars do not believe that he held, see Ezio Levi (423–26). For a review of Poeta's associations with the high nobility, see Lorenzo Rubio González (104–5) and Levi (420–23).

4. Two exceptions discussed by Scholberg (347–49) are the Old Christian poets Juan de Dueñas and Suero de Ribera.

5. I interpret the term "Macán" as a derivative of the biblical term for the name given by Jacob to the place where he receives a visit from an angel of God, in English "Mahanaim" (Gen. 32.2). By extension, I interpret the phrase "linaje de Macán" to refer to an individual who is a desdendant of Jacob, that is, a Jew. All biblical references are to the King James Version.

6. Scholberg explains that the term "perdonança" "[d]ebe de referirse a uno de los períodos de gracia durante los que los conversos o heréticos debían reconciliarse con la Iglesia" ([m]ust refer to one of the periods of grace during which *conversos* or heretics could reconcile themselves with the Church) (342, note 67). Augusto Cortina (*Jorge Manrique* xxii) attributes this poem to Pedro Manrique.

7. The phrase "bula del Padre Santo" probably refers to the general indulgence issued by Pope Paul II in 1470 (Rubio González 104).

8. "Talmud" is the name of the code of Jewish civil and religious laws not included in the Pentateuch.

9. As Rodríguez Puértolas explains, "hierro" is a reference to "la lanza que hirió el costado de Cristo en la cruz" (the lance that wounded the flank of Christ [while] on the Cross) and "bezerro" is an allusion to the Golden Calf depicted in Exodus 32 (*Poesía crítica* 291, notes 17 and 20, respectively).

10. "Tora" is synonymous with Pentateuch.

11. The phrase "caçuela con berenjena" refers to a food that "Judíos y musulmanes eran muy aficionados a comer" (Jews and Muslims were very fond of eating) (Rodríguez Puértolas, *Poesía crítica* 291, note 35).

12. Rodríguez Puértolas provides the following explanation for the terms "ataifor" and "adafina": "*ataifor*, plato hondo; es vocablo de origen árabe. *Adafina*, la comida preparada por los judíos el viernes, para ser consumida el Sábado" (*ataifor*, a deep dish; a word of Arab origin. *Adafina*, the food prepared by Jews on Friday in order to be consumed on Saturday) (*Poesía crítica* 291, note 40). With regard to the last term, in *Retrato de la Lozana andaluza* Rampín declares, "¿No veis que todos éstos son judíos, y es mañana sábado, que hacen el adafina?" (244).

13. The term "raéz," according to Jaraulde Pou, "tiene dos acepciones básicas, la del texto 'fácil,' y la de 'ignominioso' o 'vil'" (has two common meanings, the one from the text "easy" and also "ignominious" or "vile") (*Cancionero de obras* 87, note 14).

14. Jaraulde Pou (*Cancionero de obras* 87, note 16) mentions the presence of biblical allusions in this poem.

15. The term "Yahudí" is a Spanish transcription of the Hebrew term for "Jew."

16. The second person plural conjugation was used as a form of respect in order to refer to a single subject, as does the verb "entenderéys," which refers to Poeta, and to multiple subjects, as does the verb "entendáys," which refers to Poeta and "este judío." This dual function of the second person plural conjugation continued in spoken Spanish (Lloyd 359), and in literature (Lapesa 397), through the sixteenth century.

Chapter 4. *Converso* Literature and Early Castilian Humanism

1. See "Dissemination: Time, Narrative and the Margins of the Modern Nation" (Bhabha 139–70).

2. See Luis Gil Fernández and Nicholas Round.

3. See Ottavio di Camillo, José Antonio Maravall, Peter Russell, and Domingo Ynduráin.

4. In his analysis of the humanistic attitude of Pérez de Guzmán and Alonso de Cartagena, Francisco López Estrada interprets this moral and national character as a "humanismo moral, de raíces senequistas e hispánicas; bíblicas y por tanto universales; con glorificación del retiro, del apartamiento, de la áscesis" (moral humanism, of Senecan and Hispanic roots; biblical and as such universal; with a glorification of solitude, seclusion, and ascesis) (318–19).

5. See Castro (*Aspectos*), Márquez Villanueva ("The Converso Problem"; *Investigaciones*), and Carlos Moreno Hernández ("Algunos aspectos"; *Pero Guillén*; "Pero Guillén de Segovia").

6. See Sicroff (61–85) and Netanyahu (*The Origins* 528–77) for a discussion of the *Defensorium* in this context.

7. See Netanyahu for a discussion of the theme of nobility in the *Defensorium* (*The Origins* 554–69).

8. For a review of Cartagena's political and ecclesiastical careers, see Netanyahu (*The Origins* 517–27).

9. On Valera's *converso* lineage, see Marcelino Amasuno Sárraga.

10. See Gerli ("Performing Nobility") for an examination of this issue.

11. For biographical studies of Guillén, see Casas Homs's introduction to the *La gaya ciencia* (Guillén xiii–xx), Cummins (13–21), and Moreno Hernández ("Pero Guillén" 27–30), who posits that Guillén came from a family of Sevillian *conversos* that adopted Christianity "a finales del siglo XIV o principios del XV, en el comienzo de las grandes persecuciones contra los judíos" (near the end of the fourteenth or at the beginning of the fifteenth century, during the beginning of the great wave of anti-Jewish persecution) ("Pero Guillén" 27). For the most comprehensive studies of Álvarez Gato and Cota, including the details regarding their *converso* ancestries, see Márquez Villanueva (*Investigaciones*) and Francisco Cantera Burgos (*El poeta*), respectively.

12. For more on Carrillo's opposition to anti-*converso* discrimination, see Kamen (*The Spanish Inquisition* 32–33), Liss (166), and Sicroff (106–7).

13. Blecua defines the phrase "ommes de fación" as "hombres de armas" (men of arms) (Pulgar 111, note 3).

14. See Moreno Hernández ("Algunos aspectos"; *Pero Guillén*; "Pero Guillén de Segovia") for discussions of Carrillo's literary circle. Other *conversos* who are thought to have been associated with the group include Pero Díaz de Toledo, Juan de Mazuela, and Antón de Montoro (Moreno Hernández, *Pero Guillén* 34).

15. Pulgar's reference to "propriedades de aguas e de yerbas, e otros secretos de natura," which includes the practices of magic and alchemy, may be understood to be representative of Carrillo's humanistic views inasmuch as alchemy was an activity associated with humanism during the Renaissance (Garin 199–216).

16. Márquez Villanueva (*Investigaciones* 202) establishes that Álvarez Gato composed his own rubrics. See Márquez Villanueva (*Investigaciones* 292–94, 320–22) for a discussion of the influence of Pauline thought on Álvarez Gato's prose.

17. For a discussion of the influence of Seneca on Cartagena, Díaz de Toledo, and Rojas, see Louise Fothergill-Payne.

18. Márquez Villanueva discusses the influence of Seneca, "[e]l único autor clásico que Álvarez Gato conocía a fondo" ([t]he only classical author that Álvarez Gato knew well) (*Investigaciones* 182), on other poems and on Álvarez Gato's prose (*Investigaciones* 182–89, 310–12, 314–15, 318–21).

19. The term "vngnata" is, I submit, a poor transcription of "pugnante." The phrase "vngnata vileza" would therefore mean "quarrelsome vileness" in English.

Chapter 5. The Deification of Queen Isabel the Catholic in *Converso* Poetry

1. For discussions of this literary attitude toward Enrique IV, see Rodríguez Puértolas (*Poesía crítica; Poesía de protesta*) and Scholberg (242–56). Rodríguez-

Puértolas attributes the "Coplas de Mingo Revulgo" to (the *converso*) Fray Íñigo de Mendoza ("Sobre el autor").

2. The term "cochadores" may be related to "coceador," which is used literally to describe an animal that kicks and which may be employed figuratively in Valera's text in order to refer to public officials who instigate trouble.

3. Márquez Villanueva (*Investigaciones* 19–21) discusses the effect that the incarceration of Pedrarias had on the poetry of Álvarez Gato. The event occurred in 1466, during the civil war that resulted in the symbolic deposition of Enrique, and was actually part of a scheme designed to attract Pedrarias to the side of (Enrique's half-brother) Alfonso. About Alfonso's political attitude toward the *conversos*, Netanyahu writes: "Under the rule of Don Alfonso, therefore, Marrano security seemed to be assured more or less to the conversos' satisfaction, and consequently they could not be suspected of looking to King Enrique for protection" (*The Origins* 770). However, Netanyahu recognizes that this "security" was transient and began to disappear with the popular anti-*converso* uprising of 1467 in Toledo.

4. Mendoza was a great-grandson of Pablo de Santa María, who converted to Christianity in 1391 (Rodríguez Puértolas, *Fray Íñigo* x).

5. Like Mendoza, Pedro also traces his *converso* lineage to Pablo de Santa María. See Juan Bautista Avalle-Arce for the most comprehensive biographical study on Pedro de Cartagena.

6. See Cohen, Netanyahu (*The Origins* 727–28), and Rodríguez Puértolas (*Fray Íñigo* xi) for more on the attitude of the Franciscan order toward the Jews.

7. Rodríguez Puértolas ("Notas" 77) dates the poem between 1476 and 1479.

8. Rodríguez Puértolas (*Fray Íñigo* 281, note 1) explains that the phrase "por culpa de una muger" alludes to the biblical figure of Eve.

9. Menéndez Pelayo (*Orígenes* 31, note 1) based his supposition on an anecdote in which the author of the *Pasión trobada*, a religious poem composed by San Pedro, is called a "confeso" (a term synonymous with *converso*).

10. For some of the problems with Whinnom's conclusions, see Márquez Villanueva ("*Cárcel*" 199, note 6).

11. Although *Tractado* was not printed until 1491 (San Pedro, *Obras I* 44), Márquez Villanueva posits that the work was originally written "poco después de 1477" (shortly after 1477) ("*Cárcel*" 197). Whinnom, who suggests that *Tractado* was originally written around 1480, believes that the poem dedicated to Isabel may have been composed as early as 1479 (San Pedro, *Obras I* 46–47).

12. See Félix Herrero Salgado for more on parallelism in medieval Spanish literature.

13. Lida de Malkiel classifies this use of divine imagery as a "hipérbole sagrada":

esta hipérbole sagrada no es, en las postrimerías del siglo XV español, accidente de decadencia—como lo es en el resto de Europa—, sino elemento dos veces castizo, por su antigua raíz medieval y por su entronque con la irrupción de los conversos en la sociedad cristiana. ("La hipérbole sagrada" 305–6) [this sacred hyperbole is not, toward the end of the fifteenth century in Spain, an accident of (religious) decadence—as it is in the rest of Europe—, but genuinely Spanish for its ancient medieval roots and for its tie to the entrance of *conversos* into Christian society.]

14. Jones arrives at a similar conclusion with regard to Montoro's poem: "Me parece probable que la canción se escribiera poco tiempo después de la ascensión de la reina al trono y antes de 1478, cuando la fundación de la Inquisición en Castilla echó por tierra las esperanzas de tolerancia que Montoro abrigaba" (It seems probable to me that the poem was written a short time after the ascension to the throne of the queen and before 1478, when the establishment of the Inquisition in Castile dashed Montoro's hope for tolerance) (56–57). It should be noted that Jones does mention a poem by Tapia in which an indirect allusion to the divine status of Isabel is made: "porque vos sola nascistes / tan hermosa que hezistes / erejes a los que os miran" (60). Since little is known about Tapia, the *converso* poets stand out as the only identifiable writers who use divine imagery in their depictions of Isabel.

15. For discussions of fifteenth-century Spanish pro-feminist literature, see Gerli ("La 'religión del amor'"), who focuses on the amalgam between Christian and profane motifs and concludes that "el debate pro- y antifeminista de la literatura castellana del siglo XV tiene bases éticas y religiosas además de puramente literarias" (the pro- and anti-feminist debate in Castilian literature of the fifteenth century has an ethical and religious foundation in addition to the purely literary one) (86); Lida de Malkiel, who reviews "[l]a trayectoria del motivo de la dama como obra excelsa de Dios" (the trajectory of the treatment of the lady as the sublime creation of God) ("La dama" 251) from its origins through modern times in European letters; Teresa Irastortza, who believes that *cancionero* poets deified women in order to assert their male superiority; and Jacob Ornstein (12–22), who underscores the prominence of fifteenth-century Spanish pro-feminism.

Chapter 6. Rodrigo Cota's "Diálogo entre el Amor y un Viejo": A *Converso* Lament

1. A similar observation about Cota's poem is made by Salvador Martínez ("*El Viejo, el Amor y la Hermosura*" 325).

2. While "Diálogo" has escaped critical scrutiny regarding its possible *converso* meaning, other aspects of the poem have been analyzed on several occasions. For such analyses, see Aragone (Cota 12–61), Carlos Alvar, Alan Deyermond ("The Use of Animal Imagery"), Joseph Gillet, and Richard Glenn.

3. Individuals with the surname Cota mentioned in the Sentencia-Estatuto include López Fernández Cota and Juan Fernández Cota. The relationships between these two men and the poet have not yet been established. Although there is no specific mention in the Sentencia-Estatuto of Cota's father, Alonso is almost certainly referred to in connection with Álvaro de Luna: "que los dichos conversos viven e tratan sin temor de Dios, e otrosí han mostrado e muestran ser enemigos de la dicha cibdad. . . . e que notoriamente a su instancia y prosecución e solicitación

estuvo puesto real sobre la dicha cibdad contra nosotros por el condestable Don Álvaro de Luna" (Benito Ruano, *Toledo* 193).

4. See Cantera Burgos (*El poeta* 44–53) for more on Dr. Cota.

5. The reason for Juan Cota's inclusion on this list is not identified in Fidel Fita's study.

6. For more information on these lists of Judaizers, see Cantera Burgos (*Judaizantes*). Not all the relationships between the Cotas mentioned on these lists and the poet have been established.

7. This decree, number 1725 in Pilar León Tello's catalogue (2:605), is located in the Toledo cathedral. For a discussion of the decree, the poet's condemnation (which most likely occurred between 1497 and 1499), and his probable acquittal, see Gregory B. Kaplan ("Subverting a Critical Myth"). It is interesting to note that for many years scholars mistakenly placed Cota on the side of the persecutors rather than the persecuted. For example, Cortina writes that Cota turned against his fellow *conversos* (and the Jews): "no sólo abjuró; sentía, o demostraba, odio a los judíos. Para no inspirar dudas, osó asumir una actitud odiosa: fue aliado de los degolladores de conversos" (he not only renounced [his Jewish heritage]; he felt and demonstrated hatred toward Jews. So as not to inspire doubts, he dared to assume a hateful posture: he was an ally of those who persecuted *conversos*) ("El 'Diálogo'" 358). Critical attitudes such as Cortina's have resulted in part from a misinterpretation of Cota's satirical poem, the "Epitalamio burlesco." The poem has been mistakenly perceived as one that attacks all the *conversos*, rather than as one that—as the text of the work clearly demonstrates—specifically targets certain members of the Arias Dávila family as a result of a dispute between them and the Cotas.

8. The omission of the name "Cota" in favor of "Sánches de Toledo" occurs in a document dated November 30, 1526, which Gómez-Menor includes in his study (150–51) with the following rubric: "Poder otorgado por Juan de Sandoval y Martín de Alarcón, hermanos, hijos de Rodrigo Sánchez de Toledo, para la cobranza de los bienes que quedaron de Nicolás Fajardo, su hermano." Although there is evidence that during his life the poet was called Ruy Sánchez de Toledo, the use of the surname Cota was much more common (Cantera Burgos, *El poeta* 21). The point I stress here is that the poet's children would have intentionally concealed the surname Cota because this was the surname that had been employed in the decree that refers to the poet as a *condenado*.

9. For more on the surname Maguaque, see Cantera Burgos ("Maguaque").

10. Montoro's reference to Cota as "coronista / del señor Rey de Çeçilla" (Ciceri 173) establishes that the poem could not have been written before 1474, when King Ferdinand became ruler of Sicily (Ciceri 173, note 244–45).

11. See "Título 21" ("De los caballeros et de las cosas que les conviene de facer") of the second "Partida" (Alfonso X 2:197–219).

12. Kamen (*The Spanish Inquisition* 188–89) illustrates this point by providing a description of a Toledan auto-de-fé in 1486 at which 750 prisoners were judged during a span of several hours.

13. *Diccionario de autoridades,* 2d ed., s.v. "estrecha."

14. In his *Diccionario crítico* Joan Corominas explains this abbreviated form: "En la Edad Media es corriente la forma popular *liña*" (s.v. "liña").

15. Gillet postulates that Cota's poem "was probably written between 1470 and 1480" (264). Cantera Burgos does not offer any more information: "El Diálogo, en opinión de Joseph E. Gillet, fue probablemente escrito entre 1470 y 1480" (The "Diálogo," in the opinion of Joseph E. Gillet, was probably written between 1470 and 1480) (*El poeta* 72). Aragone (Cota 11) concurs with Leandro Fernández de Moratín (179) that the poem was composed around 1470, although she admits that there is no evidence to support this theory (Cota 11, note 5).

16. Faur speaks of this royal decree as the "central theme" (63) of *La vida de Lazarillo de Tormes,* which he interprets as a *converso* work (61–70).

17. Cortina ("Rodrigo Cota" 151) also notes that the poet was called "Rodrigo Cota el Viejo."

Chapter 7. *Cárcel de amor* and *Celestina* as *Converso* Laments

1. For a recent printing of the Edict of Expulsion, see Alcalá (125–29).

2. According to Whinnom, "es de suponer que San Pedro está aludiendo a las novelas de caballerías; pero también parecería una historia vieja porque tales lides formales delante del rey ya no tenían lugar en España" (presumably San Pedro is alluding to the novels of chivalry; but it would also seem to be an old-fashioned story because those types of formal combats before the king no longer took place in Spain) (San Pedro, *Obras I* 117, note 119).

3. Whinnom explains that "tu natural" means "tu súbdito o vasallo por derecho" (your subject or vassal by right) (San Pedro, *Obras I* 120, note 123).

4. Without entering into detail, Márquez Villanueva considers that this passage "podría usarse para definir la limpieza de sangre" (could be used in order to define purity of blood) (*"Cárcel"* 194).

5. Although the issue of marriage does not surface in the work, this is Leriano's goal according to Bruce Wardropper.

6. Márquez Villanueva also recognizes this notion (*"Cárcel"* 198).

7. See Nepaulsingh (29–34) for a discussion of this facet of Maimonides' work.

8. Smith is referring specifically to the studies by Garrido Pallardó and Martínez Miller.

9. Márquez Villanueva also comments on the relationship between the text and Rojas's *converso* status: "*La Celestina* puede ser entendida a la luz de la experiencia trascendente del primer grupo generacional judeoconverso que ha de sufrir una serie de difíciles iniciaciones (sexual, universitaria, social, religiosa, política) coloreadas por el trauma de la institucionalización definitiva del Santo Oficio" (*Celestina* can be understood in the light of the transcendent experience of the first generational group of *conversos,* who have to suffer a series of difficult initiations [sexual, universitarian, social, religious, political] colored by the trauma of the definitive institutionalization of the Holy Office) (*Orígenes* 141).

10. Of course, the poet discussed at length in the previous chapter, Rodrigo Cota, is twice named by Rojas (70, 74) as one of two possible authors (the other being Juan de Mena) of what scholars currently accept as *auto* 1. The similarities between "Diálogo" and *Celestina* have been studied on several occasions by scholars such as F. Castro Guisasola (178–80), Martínez ("Cota y Rojas"), and Severin.

Works Cited

El Abencerraje. Ed. Francisco López Estrada. 9th ed. Madrid: Cátedra, 1993.

Alcalá, Ángel, ed. *Judíos. Sefarditas. Conversos: La expulsión de 1492 y sus consecuencias (Ponencias del Congreso Internacional celebrado en Nueva York en noviembre de 1992).* Valladolid: Ámbito, 1995.

Alcalá, Ángel, and Jacobo Sanz. *Vida y muerte del príncipe don Juan: Historia y literatura.* Valladolid: Junta de Castilla y León, Consejería de Educación y Cultura, 1999.

Alfonso X el Sabio. *Las Siete Partidas del rey don Alfonso el Sabio.* 3 vols. Madrid: Atlas, 1972.

Alonso, Álvaro, ed. *Poesía de cancionero.* 2d ed. Madrid: Cátedra, 1991.

Alvar, Carlos. "La 'vaquilla,' el 'soliman' y otras cuestiones del 'Diálogo entre el amor y un viejo.'" *Revista de filología española* 58 (1976): 69–79.

Amasuno Sárraga, Marcelino. *Alfonso Chirino, un médico de monarcas castellanos.* Salamanca: Junta de Castilla y León, 1993.

Arbós, Cristina. "Los cancioneros castellanos del siglo XV como fuente para la historia de los judíos españoles." In *Jews and Conversos: Studies in Society and the Inquisition.* Proceedings of the Eighth World Congress of Jewish Studies Held at the Hebrew University of Jerusalem, August 16–21, 1981, ed. Yosef Kaplan, 74–82. Jerusalem: Hebrew University Magnes Press, 1982.

Artiles Rodríguez, Jenaro, ed. *Obras completas* (of Juan Álvarez Gato). Madrid: Blass, 1928.

Asensio, Eugenio. *La España imaginada de Américo Castro.* 2d ed. Barcelona: Crítica, 1992.

Avalle-Arce, Juan Bautista. "Cartagena, poeta del *Cancionero general.*" *Boletín de la Real Academia Española* 47 (1967): 287–310.

Ayllón, Cándido. *La perspectiva irónica de Fernando de Rojas.* Madrid: Porrúa Turanzas, 1984.

Azáceta, José María, ed. *Poesía cancioneril.* Barcelona: Plaza y Janés, 1984.

Baer, Yitzhak. *A History of the Jews in Christian Spain.* 2 vols. Philadelphia: Jewish Publication Society, 1992.

Barrientos, Fray Lope de. "Contra algunos zizañadores de la nación de los conuertidos del pueblo de Israel." Ed. Fr. Luis G. A. Getino. *Anales salmantinos: Vida y obras de Fr. Lope de Barrientos* 1 (1927): 180–204.

Barthes, Roland. *Mythologies.* Trans. Annette Lavers. New York: Hill and Wang, 1972.

Benito Ruano, Eloy. *Los orígenes del problema converso.* Barcelona: Albir, 1976.

———. *Toledo en el siglo XV: Vida política.* Madrid: Consejo Superior de Investigaciones Científicas, 1961.

Berceo, Gonzalo de. *Milagros de Nuestra Señora.* Ed. Michael Gerli. 5th ed. Madrid: Cátedra, 1991.

Bernáldez, Andrés. *Historia de los reyes católicos don Fernando y doña Isabel.* In *Crónicas de los reyes de Castilla,* comp. Cayetano Rosell, vol. 3, 567–773. Biblioteca de autores españoles 70. Madrid: Atlas, 1953.

Bhabha, Homi K. *The Location of Culture.* New York: Routledge, 1994.

Camillo, Ottavio di. *El humanismo castellano del siglo XV.* Trans. Manuel Lloris. Valencia: Fernando Torres, 1976.

Cancionero castellano del siglo XV. Vol. 2. Ed. R. Foulché-Delbosc. Nueva biblioteca de autores españoles 22. Madrid: Bailly-Bailliere, 1915.

Cancionero de Gómez Manrique. Ed. and intro. Antonio Paz y Melia. 2 vols. Madrid: A. Pérez Dubrull, 1885.

Cancionero de obras de burlas provocantes a risa. Ed. Pablo Jauralde Pou and Juan Alfredo Bellón Cazabán. Madrid: Akal, 1974.

Cancionero general. Ed. Antonio Rodríguez-Moñino. Madrid: Real Academia Española, 1958.

Cantera Burgos, Francisco. *Judaizantes del arzobispado de Toledo habilitados por la Inquisición en 1496 y 1497.* Madrid: Universidad de Madrid, 1969.

———. "Maguaque, remoquete de Rodrigo Cota y otros detalles acerca de éste." *Sefarad* 30 (1970): 339–47.

———. *El poeta Ruy Sánchez Cota (Rodrigo Cota) y su familia de judíos conversos.* Madrid: Universidad de Madrid, 1970.

Carpenter, Dwayne E. *Alfonso X and the Jews: An Edition of and Commentary on Siete Partidas 7.24 "De los judíos."* Berkeley: University of California Press, 1986.

Cartagena, Alonso de. *Alonso de Cartagena y el* Defensorium unitatis christianae. Trans., intro., and notes Guillermo Verdín Díaz. Oviedo: Universidad de Oviedo, n.d.

———. *Discurso.* In *Prosistas castellanos del siglo XV,* ed. Mario Penna, 205–33. Madrid: Atlas, 1959.

Castro, Américo. *Aspectos del vivir hispánico: Espiritualismo, mesianismo, actitud personal en los siglos XIV al XVI.* Santiago de Chile: Cruz del Sur, 1949.

———. *De la edad conflictiva.* Madrid: Taurus, 1961.

———. *España en su historia: Cristianos, moros y judíos.* 3d ed. Barcelona: Crítica, 1983.

————. *La realidad histórica de España.* México, D.F.: Porrúa, 1954.

————. *The Structure of Spanish History.* Trans. Edmund L. King. Princeton: Princeton University Press, 1954.

Castro Guisasola, Francisco. *Observaciones sobre las fuentes literarias de* La Celestina. 1924. Madrid: Consejo Superior de Investigaciones Científicas, 1973.

Ciceri, Marcella, ed. *Antón de Montoro: Cancionero.* Intro. and notes Julio Rodríguez Puértolas. Salamanca: Universidad de Salamanca, 1991.

Cohen, Jeremy. *The Friars and the Jews: The Evolution of Medieval Anti-Judaism.* Ithaca: Cornell University Press, 1983.

Las "Coplas de Mingo Revulgo." Ed. Vivana Brodey. Madison: Hispanic Seminary of Medieval Studies, 1986.

Corominas, Joan. *Diccionario crítico etimológico castellano e hispánico.* 4 vols. Madrid: Gredos, 1980.

Cortina, Augusto. "El 'Diálogo entr'el Amor y vn Viejo.'" *Boletín de la Academia Argentina de Letras* 1, no. 4 (1933): 319–71.

————. "Rodrigo Cota." *Revista de la biblioteca, archivo y museo* 6 (1929): 151–65.

————, ed. and intro. *Jorge Manrique: Cancionero.* 2d ed. Madrid: Espasa-Calpe, 1941.

Cota, Rodrigo. *Diálogo entre el Amor y un Viejo.* Ed. Elisa Aragone. Florence: Le Monnier, 1961.

Cotarelo, Emilio. "Nuevos y curiosos datos biográficos del famoso y novelista Diego de San Pedro." *Boletín de la Real Academia Española* 14 (1927): 305–26.

Crónica del rey don Enrique tercero de Castilla é de León. In *Crónicas de los reyes de Castilla,* comp. Cayetano Rosell, vol. 2, 161–271. Biblioteca de autores españoles 68. Madrid: Hernando, 1930.

Culler, Jonathan. *Literary Theory: A Very Short Introduction.* Oxford: Oxford University Press, 1997.

Cummins, John G. "Pero Guillén de Segovia y el ms. 4.114." *Hispanic Review* 41 (1973): 6–32.

Delicado, Francisco. *Retrato de la Lozana andaluza.* 2d ed. Ed. Claude Allaigre. Madrid: Cátedra, 1994.

Deyermond, Alan. Preliminary study. In *Diego de San Pedro: Cárcel de amor,* ed. Carmen Parrilla. Barcelona: Crítica, 1995.

————. "The Use of Animal Imagery in Cota's *Diálogo* and in Two Imitations." In *Études de philologie romane et d'histoire littéraire offertes à Jules Horrent à l'occasion de son soixantiéme anniversaire,* ed. Jean Marie D'Heur and Nicoletta Cherubini. Liège: n.p., 1980.

Díaz de Toledo, Fernán. "Instrucción del Relator para el obispo de Cuenca, a favor de la nación hebrea." In *Defensorium unitatis christianae,* by Alonso de Cartagena, ed. P. Manuel Alsonso, 343–56. Madrid: Consejo Superior de Investigaciones Científicas, 1943.

Diccionario de autoridades. 3 vols. Madrid: Gredos, 1990.

Domínguez Ortiz, Antonio. *La clase social de los conversos en Castilla en la edad moderna*. Madrid: Consejo Superior de Investigaciones Científicas, 1955.

———. *Los judeoconversos en España y América*. Madrid: Istmo, 1971.

———. *Los judeoconversos en la España moderna*. Madrid: Mapfre, 1992.

Espina, Alonso de. *Fortalitium fidei contra Judaeos*. Lyon, 1511.

Faur, José. *In the Shadow of History: Jews and Conversos at the Dawn of Modernity*. Albany: State University of New York Press, 1992.

Fernández de Oviedo y Valdés, Gonzalo. *Libro de la cámara real del príncipe don Juan*. Ed. J. M. Escudero de la Peña. Madrid: Sociedad de Bibliófilos Españoles, 1870.

Fita, Fidel. "La Inquisición toledana. Relación contemporánea de los autos y autillos que celebró desde el año 1485 hasta el de 1501." *Boletín de la Real Academia Española* 11 (1887): 289–322.

Fothergill-Payne, Louise. *Seneca and* Celestina. New York: Cambridge University Press, 1988.

Freund, Scarlett, and Teofilo F. Ruiz. "Jews, *Conversos,* and the Inquisition in Spain, 1391–1492: The Ambiguities of History." In *Jewish-Christian Encounters over the Centuries: Symbiosis, Prejudice, Holocaust, Dialogue,* ed. Marvin Perry and Frederick M. Schweitzer, 169–95. New York: Peter Lang, 1994.

Frye, Northrop. *Anatomy of Criticism: Four Essays*. Princeton: Princeton University Press, 1957.

García de Mora, Marcos. "Memorial," ed. Eloy Benito Ruano. In Eloy Benito Ruano, *Los orígenes del problema converso,* 103–32. Barcelona: Albir, 1976.

Garin, Eugenio. *La revolución cultural del renacimiento*. Trans. Domènec Bergada. Barcelona: Crítica, 1981.

Garrido Pallardó, Fernando. *Los problemas de Calisto y Melibea y el conflicto de su autor*. Figueras: Canigó, 1957.

Gerli, E. Michael. "Performing Nobility: Mosén Diego de Valera and the Poetics of *Converso* Identity." *La corónica* 25, no. 1 (1996): 19–36.

———. "La 'religión del amor' y el antifeminismo en las letras castellanas del siglo XV." *Hispanic Review* 58 (1981): 65–86.

Gil Fernández, Luis. *Panorama social del humanismo español (1500–1800)*. Madrid: Alhambra, 1981.

Gillet, Joseph. "Las ochavas en cadena: A proverb in Rodrigo Cota and Diego Sánchez de Badajoz." *Romance Philology* 6 (1952–53): 264–67.

Gilman, Stephen. *The Spain of Fernando de Rojas: The Intellectual and Social Landscape of* La Celestina. Princeton: Princeton University Press, 1972.

Gitlitz, David. *Secrecy and Deceit: The Lives of Crypto-Jews*. Philadelphia: Jewish Publication Society, 1996.

Glenn, Richard. "Rodrigo Cota's 'Diálogo entre el amor y un viejo': Debate or Drama?" *Hispania* 48 (1965): 51–56.

Gómez-Menor, José. "Una monja y un indiano hijos de Rodrigo Cota." *Sefarad* 32 (1972): 148–52.

Gracián, Baltasar. *Obras completas*. Ed. Arturo del Hoyo. Madrid: Aguilar, 1960.

Guillén de Segovia, Pero. *La gaya ciencia.* Vol 1. Ed. J. M. Casas Homs. Madrid: Consejo Superior de Investigaciones Científicas, 1962.

Herrero Salgado, Félix. *Narraciones de la España medieval.* Madrid: Magisterio Español, 1968.

Hutcheson, Gregory S. "Inflecting the *Converso* Voice." *La corónica* 25, no. 1 (1996): 3–5.

Irastortza, Teresa. "La caracterización de la mujer a través de su descripción física en cuatro cancioneros del siglo XV." *Anales de literatura española* 5 (1986–87): 189–218.

Johnson, Paul. *A History of the Jews.* New York: Harper and Row, 1987.

Jones, R. O. "Isabel la Católica y el amor cortés." *Revista de literatura* 21 (1962): 55–64.

Kamen, Henry. *Inquisition and Society in Spain in the Sixteenth and Seventeenth Centuries.* London: George Weidenfeld and Nicolson, 1985.

———. *The Spanish Inquisition.* New York: New American Library, 1965.

———. *The Spanish Inquisition: A Historical Revision.* New Haven: Yale University Press, 1998.

Kaplan, Gregory B. "'Como non deben seer apremiados los judíos que se tornan cristianos': The *Sentencia-Estatuto* and the Legacy of Alfonso X, el Sabio's *Siete Partidas.*" *Quaderni ibero-americani* 83–84 (1998): 33–49.

———. "Rodrigo Cota's 'Diálogo entre el Amor y un Viejo': A '*Converso* Lament.'" *Indiana Journal of Hispanic Literatures* 8 (1996): 7–30.

———. "In Search of Salvation: The Deification of Queen Isabel la Católica in *Converso* Poetry." *Hispanic Review* 66 (1998): 289–308.

———. "Subverting a Critical Myth: Rodrigo de Cota and the Spanish Inquisition." *Journal of Unconventional History* 8, no. 3 (1997): 49–66.

———. "Toward the Establishment of a Christian Identity: The *Conversos* and Early Castilian Humanism." *La corónica* 25, no. 1 (1996): 34–49.

King, Margaret L. *Women of the Renaissance.* Chicago: University of Chicago Press, 1991.

Ladero Quesada, M. A. "Los judíos en el arrendamiento de impuestos." *Cuadernos de historia* 6 (1975): 417–39.

Lapesa, Rafael. *Historia de la lengua española.* 9th ed. Madrid: Gredos, 1988.

Lea, Henry C. *A History of the Inquisition in Spain.* 4 vols. New York: Macmillan, 1906–7.

León Tello, Pilar. *Judíos de Toledo.* 2 vols. Madrid: Consejo Superior de Investigaciones Científicas, 1979.

Levi, Ezio. "Un juglar español en Sicilia (Juan de Valladolid)." In *Homenaje ofrecido a Menéndez Pidal,* 3:433–39. Madrid: Hernando, 1925.

Lida de Malkiel, María Rosa. "La dama como obra maestra de Dios." In *Estudios sobre la literatura española del siglo XV,* by María Rosa Lida de Malkiel, 179–290. Madrid: José Porrúa Turranzas, 1977.

———. "La hipérbole sagrada en la poesía castellana del siglo XV." In *Estudios sobre la literatura española del siglo XV,* by María Rosa Lida de Malkiel, 291–309. Madrid: José Porrúa Turranzas, 1977.

———. *La originalidad artística de* La Celestina. Buenos Aires: Editorial Universitaria de Buenos Aires, 1962.

Liss, Peggy K. *Isabel the Queen: Life and Times.* New York: Oxford University Press, 1992.

Llorente, Juan Antonio. *A Critical History of the Inquisition of Spain.* 1826. Williamstown, Mass.: John Lilburne, 1967.

Lloyd, Paul M. *From Latin to Spanish.* Philadelphia: American Philosophical Society, 1987.

López de Ayala, Pero. *Crónica del rey don Pedro.* In *Crónicas de los reyes de Castilla,* comp. Cayetano Rosell, vol. 1, 393–593. Biblioteca de autores españoles 66. Madrid: Atlas, 1953.

———. "Rimado de palacio." In *Poetas castellanos anteriores al siglo XV,* comp. Tomás Anonio Sánchez, 425–76. Biblioteca de autores españoles 57. Madrid: Hernando, 1925.

López Estrada, Francisco. "La retórica en las *Generaciones y semblanzas* de Fernán Pérez de Guzmán." *Revista de filología española* 30 (1946): 310–52.

Lotman, Yury. *Analysis of the Poetic Text.* Ed. and trans. D. Barton Johnson. Ann Arbor: Ardis, 1976.

MacKay, Angus. *La España de la Edad Media: Desde la frontera hasta el Imperio (1000–1500).* Trans. Angus MacKay and Salustiano Moreta. 4th ed. Madrid: Cátedra, 1991.

———. "Popular Movements and Pogroms in Fifteenth-Century Castile." *Past and Present* 55 (1972): 33–67.

———. *Spain in the Middle Ages: From Frontier to Empire, 1000–1500.* New York: St. Martin's, 1977.

Maimonides, Moses. *The Guide for the Perplexed.* Trans. M. Friedlander. London: Routledge, 1928.

Manuel, Juan. *El Conde Lucanor.* Ed. Alfonso I. Sotelo. 16th ed. Madrid: Cátedra, 1993.

Maravall, José Antonio. "El prerenacimiento del siglo XV." *Academia literaria renacentista* 3 (1983): 17–36.

Marciales, Miguel. "Carta al Profesor Stephen Gilman sobre problemas rojanos y celestinescos a propósito del libro *The Spain of Fernando de Rojas.*" Mérida, Venezuela: Universidad de los Andes, Facultad de Humanidades y Letras, 1973.

Márquez Villanueva, Francisco. "*Cárcel de amor,* novela política." *Revista de occidente* 14 (2nda época) (1966): 185–200.

———. "The Converso Problem: An Assessment." Trans. M. P. Hornik. In *Collected Studies in Honour of Américo Castro's 80th Year,* ed. M. P. Hornik, 317–33. Oxford: Lincombe Lodge, 1965.

———. "Conversos y cargos concejiles en el siglo XV." *Revista de archivos, bibliotecas y museos* 63 (1957): 503–40.

————. *Investigaciones sobre Juan Álvarez Gato: Contribución al conocimiento de la literatura castellana del siglo XV.* Madrid: Anejos del *Boletín de la Real Academia Española*, 1960.

————. "Jewish 'Fools' of the Spanish Fifteenth Century." *Hispanic Review* 50 (1982): 385–409.

————. *Orígenes y sociología del tema celestinesco.* Barcelona: Anthropos, 1993.

Martin, June Hall. *Love's Fools: Aucassin, Troilus, Calisto and the Parody of the Courtly Lover.* London: Tamesis, 1972.

Martínez, Salvador. "Cota y Rojas: Contribución al estudio de las fuentes y la autoría de *La Celestina.*" *Hispanic Review* 48 (1980): 37–55.

————. "*El Viejo, el Amor y la Hermosura* y la aparición del tema del desengaño en el teatro castellano primitivo." *Revista canadiense de estudios hispánicos* 4, no. 3 (1980): 311–28.

Martínez Miller, Orlando. *La ética judía y* La Celestina *como alegoría.* Miami: Universal, 1978.

Martz, Linda. "Converso Families in Fifteenth- and Sixteenth-Century Toledo: The Significance of Lineage." *Sefarad* 48 (1988): 117–96.

Mena, Juan de. *Laberinto de fortuna.* Ed. John G. Cummins. 5th ed. Madrid: Cátedra, 1996.

Menéndez Pelayo, Marcelino. *Orígenes de la novela.* Vol. 2. Ed. Enrique Sánchez Reyes. Santander: Aldus, 1943.

Merrell, Floyd. *A Semiotic Theory of Texts.* Berlin: Mouton de Gruyter, 1985.

Mettmann, Walter, ed. *Cantigas de Santa María.* 3 vols. Madrid: Castalia, 1986.

Montemayor, Jorge de. *Los siete libros de la Diana.* Ed. Francisco López Estrada. Madrid: Clásicos Castellanos, 1962.

Moratín, Leandro Fernández de. *Orígenes del teatro español.* In *Obras de D. Nicolás y D. Leandro Fernández Moratín,* vol.2, 147–306. Biblioteca de autores españoles 2. Madrid: Hernando, 1918.

Moreno Hernández, Carlos. "Algunos aspectos de la vida y la poesía de Pero Guillén de Segovia." *Anales de literatura española* 5 (1986–87): 329–56.

————. "Pero Guillén de Segovia y el círculo de Alfonso Carrillo." *Revista de literatura* 47 (1985): 17–49.

————, ed. and intro. *Pero Guillén: Obra poética.* Madrid: Fundación universitaria española, 1989.

Morrison, Toni. *Beloved.* New York: Knopf, 1987.

Nepaulsingh, Colbert I. *Apples of Gold in Filigrees of Silver: Jewish Writing in the Eye of the Spanish Inquisition.* New York: Holmes and Meier, 1995.

Netanyahu, Benzion. *The Marranos of Spain: From the Late Fourteenth to the Early Sixteenth Century.* New York: American Academy for Jewish Research, 1966.

————. *The Origins of the Inquisition in Fifteenth-Century Spain.* New York: Random House, 1995.

Nirenberg, David. *Communities of Violence: Persecution of Minorities in the Middle Ages.* Princeton: Princeton University Press, 1996.

O'Callaghan, Joseph F. *The Learned King: The Reign of Alfonso X of Castile.* Phila-delphia: University of Pennsylvania Press, 1993.

Ornstein, Jacob, ed. *Luis de Lucena: Repetición de amores.* Chapel Hill: University of North Carolina Press, 1954.

Orozco, Emilio. "*La Celestina:* Hipótesis para una interpretación." *Ínsula* 12 (1957): 1, 10.

Palencia, Alonso de. *Crónica de Enrique IV.* Biblioteca de autores españoles 257. Madrid: Atlas, 1973.

Parkes, James. *The Conflict of the Church and the Synagogue.* London: Soncino, 1934.

Passover Haggadah. Trans. and ed. Rabbi Nathan Goldberg. New York: Ktav, 1949.

Paz y Melia, Antonio. Introduction. *Cancionero de Gómez Manrique.* Vol 1. Madrid: A. Pérez Dubrull, 1885.

Penna, Mario, ed. *Prosistas castellanos del siglo XV.* Biblioteca de autores españoles 116. Madrid: Atlas, 1959.

Penny, Ralph. *A History of the Spanish Language.* Cambridge: Cambridge Univer-sity Press, 1991.

Pérez de Guzmán, Fernán. *La crónica del serenísimo príncipe don Juan, segundo rey deste nombre en Castilla y en León.* In *Crónicas de los reyes de Castilla,* comp. Cayetano Rosell, vol. 2, 277–695. Biblioteca de autores españoles 68. Madrid: Hernando, 1930.

Peters, Edward. *Inquisition.* Berkeley: University of California Press, 1989.

Poema de mio Cid. Edited with an introduction and notes by Colin Smith. Oxford: Clarendon, 1972.

Pulgar, Fernando del. *Claros varones.* Ed. José Manuel Blecua. Zaragoza: Ebro, 1945.

Rodríguez del Padrón, Juan. *Siervo libre de amor.* Ed. Antonio Prieto. 2d ed. Madrid: Castalia, 1985.

Rodríguez Puértolas, Julio. "El linaje de Calisto." *Hispanófila* 33 (1968): 1–6. Rpt. in *De la Edad Media a la edad conflictiva: Estudios de literatura española,* 209–16. Madrid: Gredos, 1972.

———. "Notas sobre un poema poco conocido de fray Íñigo de Mendoza." In *De la Edad Media a la edad conflictiva: Estudios de literatura española,* 73–100. Madrid: Gredos, 1972.

———. *Poesía de protesta en la Edad Media española.* Madrid: Gredos, 1968.

———. "Sobre el autor de las *Coplas de Mingo Revulgo.*" In *De la Edad Media a la edad conflictiva: Estudios de literatura española,* 121–36. Madrid: Gredos, 1972.

———, ed. and intro. *Fray Íñigo de Mendoza: Cancionero.* Madrid: Espasa Calpe, 1968.

———, ed. and intro. *Poesía crítica y satírica del siglo XV.* 3d ed. Madrid: Castalia, 1984.

Rojas, Fernando de. *La Celestina.* Ed. Dorothy S. Severin. 6th ed. Madrid: Cátedra, 1992.

Roth, Norman. *Conversos, Inquisition, and the Expulsion of the Jews from Spain.* Madison: University of Wisconsin Press, 1995.

Round, Nicholas G. "Renaissance Culture and Its Opponents in Fifteenth-Century Castile." *Modern Language Review* 57 (1962): 204–15.

Rubin, Nancy. *Isabella of Castile: The First Renaissance Queen.* New York: St. Martin's, 1991.

Rubio González, Lorenzo. "Juan de Valladolid: Un poeta de juglaría en el siglo XV." *Boletín del Departamento de Literatura Española* (Universidad de Valladolid) 6–7 (1983–84): 101–12.

Russell, Peter E. "Las armas contra las letras: Para una definición del humanismo español del siglo XV." In *Temas de* La Celestina *y otros estudios: Del* Cid *al* Quijote, by Peter E. Russell, 209–39. Trans. Alejandro Pérez. Barcelona: Ariel, 1978.

Sachar, Howard M. *Farewell España: The World of the Sephardim Remembered.* New York: Alfred A. Knopf, 1994.

San Pedro, Diego de. *Obras completas I: Tractado de amores de Arnalte y Lucenda, Sermón.* Ed. Keith Whinnom. Madrid: Castalia, 1985.

———. *Obras completas II: Cárcel de amor.* Ed. Keith Whinnom. 2d. ed. Madrid: Castalia, 1983.

———. *Tractado de amores de Arnalte y Lucenda.* In *Novela sentimental española,* ed. César Hernández Alonso, 127–202. Barcelona: Plaza y Janés, 1987.

Sánchez-Albornoz, Claudio. *España, un enigma histórico.* Vol. 2. Barcelona: Hispano Americana, 1973.

Santa Cruz, Alonso de. *Crónica de los Reyes Católicos.* Vol. 1. Ed. Juan de Mata Carriazo. Sevilla: Escuela de Estudios Hispano-Americanos de Sevilla, 1951.

Scholberg, Kenneth R. *Sátira e invectiva en la España medieval.* Madrid: Gredos, 1971.

Segunda parte del Cancionero general. Ed. Antonio Rodríguez-Moñino. Oxford: Dolphin, 1956.

Seidenspinner-Núñez, Dayle. "Inflecting the *Converso* Voice: A Commentary on Recent Theories." *La corónica* 25, no. 1 (1996): 6–18.

Serrano Poncela, Segundo. "El secreto de Melibea." *Cuadernos americanos* 17 (1958): 488–510.

Severin, Dorothy S. "Cota, His Imitator, and *La Celestina:* The Evidence Reexamined." *Celestinesca* 4 (1980): 3–8.

Sicroff, Albert A. *Los estatutos de limpieza de sangre: Controversias entre los siglos XV y XVII.* Trad. Mauro Armiño. Madrid: Taurus, 1985.

Smith, Paul Julian. *Representing the Other: "Race," Text, and Gender in Spanish and Spanish American Narrative.* Oxford: Clarendon, 1992.

Strauss, Leo. *Persecution and the Art of Writing.* Glencoe, Ill.: Free Press, 1952.

Trachtenberg, Joshua. *The Devil and the Jews: The Medieval Conception of the Jew and Its Relation to Modern Anti-Semitism.* Philadelphia: Jewish Publication Society, 1983.

"Traslado de una carta de privilegio que el rey Don Juan II dio a un hidalgo." In *Sales españolas*, 2d ed., comp. Antonio Paz y Melia, ed. Ramón Paz, 25–28. Biblioteca de autores españoles 176. Madrid: Atlas, 1964.

Valdeón Baruque, Julio. *Los judíos de Castilla y la revolución Trastámara.* Valladolid: Universidad de Valladolid, 1968.

———. "Motivaciones socioeconómicas de las fricciones entre viejocristianos, judíos y conversos." In *Judíos. Sefarditas. Conversos: La expulsión de 1492 y sus consecuencias (Ponencias del Congreso Internacional celebrado en Nueva York en noviembre de 1992)*, ed. Ángel Alcalá, 69–88. Valladolid: Ámbito, 1995.

Valera, Diego de. "Epístolas de Mosén Diego de Valera." In *Prosistas castellanos del siglo XV*, ed. Mario Penna, 3–51. Biblioteca de autores españoles 116. Madrid: Atlas, 1959.

———. *Espejo de verdadera nobleza.* In *Prosistas castellanos del siglo XV*, ed. Mario Penna, 89–113. Biblioteca de autores españoles 116. Madrid: Atlas, 1959.

Vendrell Gallostra, Francisca. "La posición del poeta Juan de Dueñas respecto a los judíos españoles de su época." *Sefarad* 18 (1958): 108–13.

Vendrell de Millás, Francisca. "Retrato irónico de un funcionario converso." *Sefarad* 28 (1968): 40–44.

La vida de Lazarillo de Tormes y de sus fortunas y adversidades. Ed. Joseph V. Ricapito. 11th ed. Madrid: Cátedra, 1983.

Wardropper, Bruce W. "El mundo sentimental de la *Cárcel de Amor*." *Revista de filología española* 37 (1953): 168–93.

Weill, Julien. "Note sur les maranes d'Espagne." *Revue des études juives* 87 (1929): 59–61.

Whinnom, Keith. *La poesía amatoria cancioneril en la época de los Reyes Católicos.* Durham, Eng.: University of Durham, 1981.

———. "Was Diego de San Pedro a *Converso*? A Re-Examination of Cotarelo's Documentary Evidence." *Bulletin of Hispanic Studies* 34 (1957): 187–200.

Wolff, Philippe. "The 1391 Pogrom in Spain: Social Crisis or Not?" *Past and Present* 50 (1971): 4–18.

Ynduráin, Domingo. *Humanismo y Renacimiento en España.* Madrid: Cátedra, 1994.

Index

Gregory B. Kaplan is associate professor of Spanish at the University of Tennessee. He specializes in literature of the Spanish Middle Ages.